Y0-CLD-352

Published by

All Sports Art and Publications, Inc.
P.O. Box 4399
East Lansing, MI 48826

Copyright 1989 by Larry Bielat ©

All rights reserved. No part of this book may be reproduced or transmitted in any form or by any means, electronic or mechanical, including photocopying, recording, or by any information storage and retrieval system, without the written permission of the Publisher, except where permitted by law.

Printed in the United States of America, 1989

WINNING WORDS OF AMERICAN BUSINESS

Compiled by Larry Bielat

Published by
ALL SPORTS ART AND PUBLICATIONS, INC
P.O. Box 4399, East Lansing, MI 48826

Layout and production of this publication conceived and performed by Richard E. Brown, Jr. and Mark F. Howe of:

Hobo Productions
P.O. Box 12004, Lansing, MI 48901

Quantity Sales

Winning Words of American Business is available at special quantity discounts when purchased in bulk by corporations, organizations, or special interest groups. Custom imprinting can also be done to fit special needs.

For details, please write:
All Sports Art and Publications, Inc.,
P.O. Box 4399, East Lansing, MI 48826.

PREFACE

This is my fifth book on motivation and inspiration. The first four were aimed at teachers, coaches, athletes, and school administrators. People in the business world ordered copies of my books and encouraged me to go through my collection and do a book for the business community.

I hope you find in this collection some words to uplift you and get your motor moving. We all have bad days and often need to hear or read some small verse or line of wisdom to refuel that energy tank. I hope my book might be what you need on some of those not so sunny days.

I wish to apologize to any authors who are not given credit for their work. My collection has been gathered for over 30 years from speeches, books, articles and often the walls of some offices. When no author was mentioned, I just copied the piece and "anonymous" got the credit.

This book is dedicated to three fine young men whom I love and respect:

James West, Jr.

Russell Davis

&

Mark Schubert

May God sit on your shoulders and guide you through life.

2/3 of Promotion is =Motion

☆ ☆ ☆ ☆ ☆

HOW TO LIVE A HUNDRED YEARS HAPPILY

1. Do not be on the outlook for ill health.
2. Keep usefully at work.
3. Have a hobby.
4. Learn to be satisfied.
5. Keep on liking people.
6. Meet adversity valiantly.
7. Meet the little problems of life with decision.
8. Above all, maintain a good sense of humor, best done by saying something pleasant every time you get a chance.
9. Live and make the present hour pleasant and cheerful. Keep your mind out of the past and keep it out of the future.

I am a Salesman

I am proud to be a **salesman** because more than any other man I, and millions of others like me, built America.

The man who builds a better mousetrap—or a better anything—would starve to death if he waited for people to beat a pathway to his door. Regardless of how good, or how needed the product or service might be, it has to be sold.

Eli Whitney was laughed at when he showed his cotton gin. Edison had to install his electric light free of charge in an office building before anyone would even look at it. The first sewing machine was smashed to pieces by a Boston mob. People scoffed at the idea of railroads.

They thought that even traveling thirty miles an hour would stop the circulation of the blood! McCormick strived for fourteen years to get people to use his reaper. Westinghouse was considered a fool for stating that he could stop a train with wind. Morse had to plead before ten Congresses before they would even look at his telegraph.

The public didn't go around demanding these things; they had to be sold! They needed thousands of salesmen, trailblazers, pioneers, people who could persuade with the same effectiveness as the inventor could invent. Salesmen took these inventions, sold the public on what these products could do, taught customers how to use them, and then taught businessmen how to make a profit from them. As a salesman I've done more to make America what it is today than any other person you know. I was just as vital in your great-great-grandfather's day as I am in yours, and I'll be just as vital in your great-great-grandson's day. I have educated more people; created more jobs; taken more drudgery from the laborer's work; given more profits to businessmen; and have given more people a fuller and richer life than anyone in history. I've dragged prices down, pushed quality up, and made it possible for you to enjoy the comforts and luxuries of automobiles, radios, electric refrigerators, televisions, and airconditioned homes and buildings. I've healed the sick, given security to the aged, and put thousands of young men and women through college. I've made it possible for inventors to invent, for factories to hum, and for ships to sail the seven seas.

How much money you find in your pay envelope next week, and whether in the future you will enjoy the luxuries of prefabricated homes, stratospheric flying airplanes, and a new world of jet propulsion and atomic power, depends on me. The loaf of bread that you bought today was on a baker's shelf because I made sure that a farmer's wheat got to a mill, that the mill made the wheat into flour, and that the flour was delivered to your baker.

Without me the wheels of industry would come to a grinding halt. And with that, jobs, marriages, politics and freedom of thought would be a thing of the past.

I AM A SALESMAN and I'm both proud and grateful that as such I serve my family, my fellow man and my country.

AUTHOR UNKNOWN

A MAN GROWS MOST TIRED STANDING STILL

☆ ☆ ☆ ☆ ☆

NEVER BE SATISFIED

☆ ☆ ☆ ☆ ☆

PAY NO ATTENTION TO WHAT THE CRITICS SAY. A STATUE HAS NEVER BEEN ERECTED IN HONOR OF A CRITIC.
— Jean Sibelius

☆ ☆ ☆ ☆ ☆

What Today Will Bring...

This is the beginning of a new day. God has given me this day to use as I will. I can waste it or use it for good. What I do today is important, because I'm exchanging a day of my life for it. When tomorrow comes this day will be gone forever, leaving in its place something I have traded for it. I want it to be gain, not loss; good, not evil; success, not failure, in order that I shall not regret the price I paid for it because the future is just a whole string of **nows**.

☆ ☆ ☆ ☆ ☆

It is not he that enters upon any career, or starts in any race, but he that runs well and perseveringly that gains the plaudits of others or the approval of his own conscience.

— Alexander Campbell

I'm Your Customer Who Never Comes Back

I'm a nice customer. All merchants know me. I'm the one who never complains, no matter what kind of service I get. When I go to a store to buy something, I don't throw my weight around. I try to be thoughtful of the other person. If I get a snooty clerk who gets nettled because I want to look at several things before I make up my mind, I'm as polite as can be; I don't believe rudeness in return is the answer.

I never kick, complain, or criticize, and I wouldn't dream of making a scene as I've seen people doing in public places. No, I'm the nice customer, but I'm also the nice customer who *never comes back*.

That's my little revenge for being abused and taking whatever you hand out, because I *know* I'm not coming back. This doesn't immediately relieve my feelings, but in the long run it's far more satisfying than blowing my top.

In fact, a nice customer like myself, multiplied by others of my kind, can ruin a business. And there are a lot of nice people just like me. When we get pushed far enough, we go to another store where they appreciate nice customers.

He laughs best, they say, who laughs last. I laugh when I see you frantically advertising to get me back, when you could have kept me in the first place with a few kind words and a smile.

Your business might be in a different town and your situation might be "different", but if business is bad, chances are good that if you change your attitude, the word will get around and I'll change from the nice customer who never comes back—and brings his friends.

SETBACKS NEVER WHIP A FIGHTER

☆ ☆ ☆ ☆ ☆

TRY AND BE THE BEST
If you can't be the pine on top of the hill, be a scrub in the valley - but be the best little scrub at the side of the hill; be a bush if you can't be a tree.

If you can't be a bush, be a bit of grass, some highway to happier make; if you can't be a muskie; then just be a bass - but be the liveliest bass in the lake.

We can't all be captains, some have to be crew; there's something for all of us here; there's big work to do; there's lesser to do; and the task we must do is near.

If you can't be a highway, then just be a trail, if you can't be a sun, be a star. It isn't by size that you win or you fail. Be the *Best* of whatever you are.

-Joe Dirk

☆ ☆ ☆ ☆ ☆

*"The surest way not to fail, is to be **determined to succeed.**"*

☆ ☆ ☆ ☆ ☆

No trial would trouble you if you knew God's purpose in sending it.

THERE IS NO SADDER SIGHT THAN A YOUNG PESSIMIST.
--MARK TWAIN

☆ ☆ ☆ ☆ ☆

WHEN THE PRESSURE'S ON
How do you act when the **pressure's on,** when the chance for victory's almost gone, when Fortune's star has refused to shine, when the ball is on your five-yard line?

How do you act when the going's rough? Does your spirit lag when breaks are tough? Or is there in you a flame that glows brighter as fiercer the battle grows?

How hard, how long will you fight the foe? That's what the world would like to know! Cowards can fight when they're out ahead! The up hill grind shows a thoroughbred!

You wish for success? Then tell me, sir, how do you act when the **pressure's on?**

☆ ☆ ☆ ☆ ☆

The Lord
sometimes takes us into troubled waters not to drown but to cleanse us...

FOOD FOR THOUGHT:

In 1923, a very important meeting was held at the Edgewater Beach Hotel in Chicago. Attending this meeting were nine of the world's most successful financiers. Those present were:

> The **president** of the *largest independent steel company*
> The **president** of the largest utility company.
> The **president** of the *largest gas company.*
> The **greatest** *wheat speculator.*
> The **president** of the *New York Stock Exchange.*
> The **president** of the *Board of International Settlements.*
> A member of the *president's cabinet.*
> The greatest "bear" on *Wall Street.*
> The head of the world's greatest monopoly.

Certainly we must admit that here were gathered a group of the world's most successful men. Men who had at least found the secret of "making money".

Twenty-five years later, let's see where these men were:

> The president of the world's largest independent steel company--**Charles Schwab**--died bankrupt after living on borrowed money for five years before his death.
> The president of the largest utility company--**Samuel Insull**--died a fugitive from justice and penniless in a foreign land.
> The president of the largest gas company--**Howard Hopson**—became insane.
> The greatest wheat speculator--**Arthur Cutten**--died insolvent abroad.
> The president of the New York Stock Exchange--**Richard Whiteney**--went to Sing-Sing Penitentiary.
> The member of the President's Cabinet--**Albert Fall**--was pardoned from prison so he could die at home.
> The greatest "bear" in Wall Street--**Jesse Livermore** --committed suicide.
> The head of the greatest monopoly—**Ivar Krueger**—committed suicide.
> The president of the Board of International Settlements—**Leon Fraser**—committed suicide.

ALL OF THESE MEN LEARNED WELL THE ART OF MAKING MONEY, BUT NOT ONE OF THEM LEARNED HOW TO LIVE. NOW - WON'T YOU STAY ANOTHER DAY AND LIVE?

A capable man on earth is more valuable than any precious deposit *under* the earth.

☆ ☆ ☆ ☆ ☆

He who works with his *hands* is a laborer. He who works with his hands and his *head* is a craftsman. He who works with his hands, his head and his *heart* is an artist. He who works with his hands, his head, his heart and his *feet* is a salesman.

☆ ☆ ☆ ☆ ☆

HE WHO HAS HEART HAS HOPE
AND
HE WHO HAS HOPE HAS EVERYTHING.
-ARABIAN PROVERB

☆ ☆ ☆ ☆ ☆

Anger is only one letter short of danger.

☆ ☆ ☆ ☆ ☆

The quality of a man's life is in direct proportion to his commitment to excellence, regardless of his chosen field of endeavor.

☆ ☆ ☆ ☆ ☆

Only a Mediocre Person Is Always at His Best.

-Somerset Maugham

One Day At A Time

☆ ☆ ☆ ☆ ☆

Everything cometh to he that waiteth, so long as he who waiteth worketh like hell while he waiteth.

☆ ☆ ☆ ☆ ☆

There are two days in every week about which we should not worry--two days which should be kept free from fear and apprehension. One of these days is **yesterday.** With its mistakes and cares, its faults and blunders, its aches and pains, yesterday has passed forever beyond our control. All the money in the world cannot bring back yesterday. We cannot undo a single act we performed. We cannot erase a single word said. Yesterday is gone!

The other day we should not worry about is **tomorrow.** With its possible adversities, its burdens, its large promise and poor performance, tomorrow is beyond our immediate control. Tomorrow's sun will rise, whether in splendor or behind a mask of clouds, but it will rise. Until it does we have no stake in tomorrow, for it is yet unborn.

This leaves only one day...**today.** Any man can fight the battles of just one day. It is when you and I add the burdens of two awful eternities - yesterday and tomorrow- that we break down. It is not necessarily the experience of *today* that disturbs one's peace of mind. It is oftentime the bitterness for something which happened yesterday and the dread of what tomorrow may bring that disturbs. Let us therefore live one day at a time.

TRYING TO SQUASH A RUMOR IS LIKE TRYING TO UNRING A BELL.

☆ ☆ ☆ ☆ ☆

Some of us will do our jobs well and some will not, but we will all be judged by only one thing - *results*.

☆ ☆ ☆ ☆ ☆

TO MISS YOUR TARGET IS NOT COMPLETE FAILURE, TO AIM LOW IS.

☆ ☆ ☆ ☆ ☆

A ship in a harbor is safe... but that is not what ships are built for!

☆ ☆ ☆ ☆ ☆

We accomplish in proportion to what we attempt.

☆ ☆ ☆ ☆ ☆

If it's worth doing at all, it's worth doing well.

Life is not easy for any of us, but it is a continued challenge. It is up to us to be cheerful and to be strong so that those who depend on us may draw strength from our example.

☆ ☆ ☆ ☆ ☆

MEMORY

Here are ten tips to improve your memory:
1) Intend to remember.
2) Understand what you are trying to remember.
3) Organize what you know into meaningful patterns.
4) Become genuinely interested in what you want to remember.
5) Use as many senses as possible.
6) Associate what you want to remember with what you know.
7) If you cannot find a logical association for a new fact, invent your own.
8) If you have a great deal to remember, spread it over a few days.
9) Review what you want to remember as often as possible.
10) The best time to memorize is at night before you go to bed.

☆ ☆ ☆ ☆ ☆

THE IMPORTANT THING IS THIS: TO BE ABLE AT ANY MOMENT TO SACRIFICE WHAT WE ARE FOR WHAT WE COULD BECOME.
                    DUBOISE

☆ ☆ ☆ ☆ ☆

The first hour of the morning is
            the rudder of the day.

☆ ☆ ☆ ☆ ☆

Character is made by what you stand for;
    Reputation by what you fall for.

You can't keep a good man down, or a bad man up.
--P.K. Thomajan

☆ ☆ ☆ ☆ ☆

It takes less time to do a **thing right** than it does to explain why you did it wrong.

☆ ☆ ☆ ☆ ☆

LEADERS have two important characteristics:
FIRST, they are going somewhere;
SECOND, they are able to persuade other people to go with them...

☆ ☆ ☆ ☆ ☆

The difference between the **wise man** and the **fool?** The **fool** says what he knows, the **wise man** knows what he says.

☆ ☆ ☆ ☆ ☆

THE QUITTER GIVES AN ALIBI,
THE MONGREL, HE GETS BLUE
THE FIGHTER GOES DOWN FIGHTING,
BUT THE THOROUGHBRED COMES THRU.

☆ ☆ ☆ ☆ ☆

When you think you're at the end of your rope, tie a knot in it and **hang on!**

☆ ☆ ☆ ☆ ☆

WE ARE ALL **MANUFACTURERS** — SOME MAKE *GOOD*, OTHERS MAKE *TROUBLE*, AND STILL OTHERS MAKE *EXCUSES*.

Men are born with two eyes and one tongue, in order that they should see twice as much as they say.
(Or two ears so we should listen twice as much as we speak.)
--C.C. Cocton

IN BUSINESS...

IT IS NOT EASY
>   To apologize,
>   To begin over,
>   To be unselfish,
>   To take advice,
>   To admit an error,
>   To face a sneer,
>   To be charitable,
>   To keep on trying,
>   To be considerate,
>   To avoid mistakes,
>   To endure success,
>   To profit by mistakes,
>   To forgive and forget,
>   To think and then act,
>   To keep out of the rut,
>   To make the best of little,
>   To subdue an unruly temper,
>   To shoulder a deserved blame,
>   To recognize the silver lining

BUT IT ALWAYS PAYS, TRY IT!

☆ ☆ ☆ ☆ ☆

THE GUY WHO GETS AHEAD, IS THE GUY WHO DOES MORE THAN IS NECESSARY -- AND KEEPS ON DOING IT.

A JOB DONE POORLY
STANDS AS A WITNESS AGAINST THE MAN WHO DID IT.

☆ ☆ ☆ ☆ ☆

A research organization polled 500 executives, asking them what traits they thought were most important in dealing with others. From the information received, these five basic **"rules"** were formulated:
1. Always give your people the credit that is rightfully theirs. To do otherwise is both morally and ethically dishonest.
2. Be courteous. Have genuine consideration for other people's feelings, wishes and situations.
3. Never tamper with the truth. Never rationalize. What you might like to believe is not necessarily the truth.
4. Be concise in your writing and talking, especially when giving instructions to others.
5. Be generous. Remember that it is the productivity of others that makes possible your executive position.

☆ ☆ ☆ ☆ ☆

Success is never permanent. Fortunately, neither is failure...

☆ ☆ ☆ ☆ ☆

MOST ANYTHING IN LIFE IS EASIER TO *GET INTO* THAN *OUT OF.*

Nothing is opened by mistake as often as one's mouth.

☆ ☆ ☆ ☆ ☆

What is the Price of Success?

To use all of your courage to force yourself to concentrate on the problem at hand, to think of it deeply and constantly, to study it from all angles and to plan.

To have a high and sustained determination to put over what you plan to accomplish, not if circumstances be favorable to its accomplishment, but in spite of all adverse circumstances which may arise. Nothing worthwhile has ever been accomplished without some obstacles to overcome.

To refuse to believe that there are any circumstances sufficiently strong to defeat you in the accomplishment of your purpose.

☆ ☆ ☆ ☆ ☆

EVERYBODY SHOULD BE PAID WHAT HE'S WORTH. NO MATTER HOW BIG A CUT HE MIGHT HAVE TO TAKE.

☆ ☆ ☆ ☆ ☆

You are today where your thoughts have brought you. You will be tomorrow where your thoughts take you.
　　　　　　　　　　--James Allen

What workers and bosses want:

I Want A Boss...

Who had something to do with hiring me and who wants me to work for him.
Who helps me when I am new to get acquainted with my job.
Who explains to me just what my job is; just what I am expected to do.
Who tells me frequently how I'm getting along - what I do well and what I don't do well - who shows me how to do better.
Who not only thinks of me for what I am but also for what I may become.
Who takes a personal interest in me and my problems.
Who listens to my ideas for making the job easier and better.
Who has something to do with my pay and does it when the time comes.
Who stands up for me when I am right.
Who is honest and four-square with me.
Who tells me about changes before they are made.
Who has personal faith and confidence in me.

**I WOULD DO MY BEST FOR A BOSS LIKE THAT!
YOU WOULD TOO!**

☆ ☆ ☆ ☆ ☆

If you deliberately plan to be less than you are capable of being, then I warn you that you'll be unhappy for the rest of your life.
                 Abraham Maslow

I Want A Worker...

Who likes his job.
Who knows his job.
Who keeps himself physically fit.
Who wants to do a day's work for a day's pay.
Who wants to get ahead.
Who is always on the job unless excused.
Who is cheerful - not sullen.
Who works safely - with due consideration for himself and his fellow workers - and gets a bang out of a job well done.
Who tries to avoid waste and cut costs.
Who looks for a better way to do the job.
Who tells the truth; who is sincere.
Who gripes little and looks forward.
Who keeps a spirit of team work.
Who asks questions when he needs help.
Who is willing to face his personal problems squarely.
Who tries to put himself in my place now and then.
Who feels that his job is a privilege, not a right.

I WOULD GIVE A WORKER LIKE THAT MY BEST!
YOU WOULD TOO!

☆ ☆ ☆ ☆

Happiness is a direction, not a place.

EXPERIENCE IS A WONDERFUL THING. IT ENABLES YOU TO RECOGNIZE A MISTAKE WHEN YOU MAKE IT AGAIN.

☆ ☆ ☆ ☆ ☆

Associate with men of good quality if you esteem your own reputation, for it's better to be alone than in bad company.

George Washington

☆ ☆ ☆ ☆ ☆

It is better to keep your mouth shut and be thought a fool, than to open it and remove all doubt.

☆ ☆ ☆ ☆ ☆

One moment of patience may ward off a great disaster; **one moment** of impatience may ruin a whole life.

☆ ☆ ☆ ☆ ☆

No horse gets anywhere until he is harnessed.
No stream ever drives anything until it is confined.
No life ever grows until
            it is focused,
                dedicated,
                      and disciplined.

☆ ☆ ☆ ☆ ☆

**Give the world the best you have
And the best will come back to you.**

FIGURE IT OUT FOR YOURSELF

Figure it out for yourself, my lad, you've all that the greatest of men have had; two arms, two hands, two legs, two eyes, and a brain to use if you would be wise. With this equipment they all began, so start from the top and say, "I can."

Look them over, the wise and the great, they take their food from a common plate, and similar knives and forks they use, with similar laces they tie their shoes. The world considers them brave and smart, but you've all they had when they made their start.

You can triumph and come to skill, you can be great if you only will. You're well equipped for what fight you choose; you have arms and legs and a brain to use, and the man who has risen great deeds to do, began his life with no more than you.

You are the handicap you must face, you are the one who must choose your place. You must say where you want to go, how much you will study the truth to know; God has equipped you for life, but He lets you decide what you want to be.

Courage must come from the soul within, the man must furnish the will to win. So figure it out for yourself, my lad, you were born with all that the great have had. With your equipment they all began, get hold of yourself and say: "I can."

☆ ☆ ☆ ☆ ☆

ANYONE WHO STOPS LEARNING IS OLD, WHETHER THIS HAPPENS AT 20 OR 80.

"GREATNESS cannot be achieved without **DISCIPLINE."**

☆ ☆ ☆ ☆ ☆

WHY ARE YOU TIRED?
We have some absolutely irrefutable statistics that show why you are tired, and brother, it's no wonder you are tired. There aren't as many people working as you may have thought, at least according to this survey.

The population of this country is 200 million, but there are 62 million over 60 years of age. That leaves 138 million to do the work. People under 21 total 94 million - that leaves 44 million to do the work. Then there are 21 million who are employed by the government, which leaves 23 million to do the work. 10 million are in the armed forces which leaves 13 million to do the work. There are 12,800,000 in the state and city offices, leaving 200,000 to do the work. 126,000 in hospitals, etc., so that leaves 74,000 to do the work. However, 62,000 bums or vagrants refuse to work so that leaves 12,000. 11,998 are in jail, which leaves **2 people** to do the work. That's you and me brother, and I'm getting tired of doing **everything myself.** (The numbers have changed. This was first published in 1958).

☆ ☆ ☆ ☆ ☆

AFTER ALL IS SAID AND DONE, THERE'S A LOT MORE *SAID* **THAN** *DONE.*

When a man is wrapped up in himself, he makes a pretty small package.

☆ ☆ ☆ ☆ ☆

Someone has compiled the following 10 excuses that are not recommended for ambitious men and women:

1. *That's the way we've always done it.*
2. *I didn't know you were in a hurry for it.*
3. *That's not in my department.*
4. *No one told me to go ahead.*
5. *I'm waiting for an OK.*
6. *How did I know this was different?*
7. *That's his job, not mine.*
8. *Wait till the boss comes back and ask him.*
9. *I forgot.*
10. *I didn't think it was important.*

☆ ☆ ☆ ☆ ☆

THE ONLY THINGS THAT EVOLVE BY THEMSELVES IN AN ORGANIZATION ARE **DISORDER, FRICTION** AND **MALPERFORMANCE**.

☆ ☆ ☆ ☆ ☆

EVERY SUCCESSFUL MAN I HAVE HEARD OF HAS DONE THE BEST HE COULD WITH THE CONDITIONS AS HE FOUND THEM, AND NOT WAITED UNTIL NEXT YEAR FOR BETTER.
　　　　　　　E.W. HOWE

DON'T WASTE TIME IN doubts and fears; spend yourself in the work before you, well assured that the right performance of this hour's duties will be the best preparation for the hours or ages that follow it.
— Emerson

☆ ☆ ☆ ☆ ☆

The Game Of Life
To each is given a bag of tools,
a shapeless mass and a book of rules,
and each must fashion ere life is flown,
a stumbling block or a stepping stone.

Isn't it strange that princes and kings
and clowns that caper in sawdust rings
and common folk like you and me
are builders of eternity?

☆ ☆ ☆ ☆ ☆

People are not **excellent** because they achieve great things, they achieve great things because they choose to be **excellent.**

☆ ☆ ☆ ☆ ☆

A pat on the back...
though only a few vertebrae removed from a kick in the pants, is miles ahead in results.

☆ ☆ ☆ ☆ ☆

When a thing is done, it's done. Don't look back, look forward to your new objective.
— Geo. C. Marshall

THE TRUE MAN

This is the sort of a man was he:
   True when it hurt him a lot to be;
   tight in a corner an' knowin' a lie
   would have helped him out,
   but he wouldn't buy
   his freedom there in so cheap a way--
   he told the truth though he had to pay.

   Honest! Not in the easy sense,
   when he needn't worry about expense,
   we'll all play square when it doesn't count and the
   sum at stake's not a large amount,
   but he was square when the times were bad,
   an' keepin' his word took all he had.

   Honor is something we all profess,
   but most of us cheat--some more, some less--
   an' the real test isn't the way we do
   when there isn't a pinch in either shoe;
   it's whether we're true to our best or not when the
   right thing's certain to hurt a lot.

That is the sort of a man was he:
   Straight when it hurt him a lot to be;
   times when a lie would have paid him well,
   no matter the cost, the truth he'd tell;
   An' he'd rather go down to a drab defeat
   than save himself if he had to cheat.
              Edgar A. Guest

☆ ☆ ☆ ☆ ☆

A PERSON IS ABOUT AS BIG AS THE THINGS THAT MAKE HIM ANGRY.

B. C. FORBES

I once asked one of America's foremost financiers what he considered the acme of business success. His reply came promptly: "To establish and place on a sound, permanent basis a business affording employment to a large number of fellow beings at wages enabling them to live in comfort and happiness."

☆ ☆ ☆ ☆ ☆

HANG TO YOUR GRIT

Don't give up hoping when the ship goes down, grab a spar or something — just refuse to drown.
Don't think you are dying just because you're hit, smile in face of danger and hang to your grit.
Folks die too easy — they sort of fade away; make a little error and give up in dismay.
Kind of man that's needed is the man of ready wit, to laugh at pain and trouble and keep up his grit.

☆ ☆ ☆ ☆ ☆

Little men with little minds and little imagination jog through life in little ruts, smugly resisting all changes which would jar their little worlds.

                                    Marie Fraser

☆ ☆ ☆ ☆ ☆

MEN SHOW THEIR CHARACTER IN NOTHING MORE CLEARLY THAN BY WHAT THEY THINK LAUGHABLE.

**THE SMALLEST GOOD DEED
IS BETTER
THAN THE GREATEST INTENTION.**

☆ ☆ ☆ ☆ ☆

The Self Esteem Credo

God made me — I was no accident.
No happenstance, I was in God's plan
and He doesn't make junk, *ever*.
I was born to be a successful human being.
I am somebody special, unique,
definitely one of a kind, and I love me.
That is essential so that I might love you, too.
I have talents, potentials;
yes, there is greatness in me
and If I harness that specialness,
then I will write my name in the
sands of time with my deeds.
Yes, I must work harder, longer,
with greater drive if I am to excel.
And I will pay that price,
for talents demand daily care and honing.
I was born in God's image and likeness
and I will strive to do God's will.

☆ ☆ ☆ ☆ ☆

**UNLESS YOU TRY TO DO SOMETHING
BEYOND WHAT YOU HAVE ALREADY
DONE AND MASTERED, YOU WILL
NEVER GROW...**

A PARROT TALKS MUCH BUT FLIES LITTLE.

☆ ☆ ☆ ☆ ☆

      The old fashioned salesman is often pictured as a fast talker, a fly-by-night operator who peddled wares of doubtful merit, a nimble-witted sharpie not far removed from bunko artist. Whatever the salesman of the past may have been, today's successful salesman is a different breed. He is a man who knows his product and his company, has faith in it, and wants to let the world know how good he thinks that product is.
Robert C. Moot

☆ ☆ ☆ ☆ ☆

He That Loses Money Loses Little
He That Loses Health Loses Much
But He That Loses Courage Loses All

☆ ☆ ☆ ☆ ☆

Thank God every morning when you get up that you have something to do which must be done, whether you like it or not. Being forced to do your best will breed in you temperance, self-control, diligence, strength of will, content and a hundred other virtues which the idle never know.

☆ ☆ ☆ ☆ ☆

IT IS A FOOLISH MAN
THAT HEARS ALL THAT HE HEARS.

Don't be afraid to take a big step if one is indicated. You can't cross a chasm in two small jumps.

☆ ☆ ☆ ☆

WHAT IT TAKES

If you have what it takes when it takes it, no matter the journey be long, you can go down the road with a smile and the heavens will ring with your song.

The world can be yours if you'll think so, at least in your mind. It will be a joy for your thoughts to feast on and a pleasure for your vision to see.

You can have it for yours if you want it, but you must open your heart to its charms, and court it as you would your sweetheart by inviting it into your arms.
    F.W. McNamara

☆ ☆ ☆ ☆

CHANCE FAVORS THE PREPARED MIND.
    - LOUIS PASTEUR

☆ ☆ ☆ ☆

Use what talents you possess...
the woods would be very silent if no birds sang there except those who sang best.

In reading the lives of great men, I found that the first victory they won was over themselves.

— *Harry S. Truman*

☆ ☆ ☆ ☆ ☆

IT CAN HAPPEN THIS WAY
by Grantland Rice

He took his turn, half-heartedly, outlining an excuse. He figured he was beaten so he couldn't see the use. But when he made his little play, it took a lucky swerve, a sudden, unexpected hop — a title-winning curve — and straightaway they exclaimed about his "courage" and his nerve.

He started in with bulldog jaw to make a winning fight. He started to see it through, as any stalwart might. But when he cut in with his play, it took a hard luck bound, and caromed as it shouldn't have on any sort of ground and so they rose and branded him a "quitter" and a "hound".

Yes, courage is a fancy word that gives us all a brace, and yellow is another term we splash about the place. But there are things behind the scenes that none of us can see, an edict from the gods of chance, whoever they may be, who set the score and laugh aloud at our philosophy.

☆ ☆ ☆ ☆ ☆

"Impossible," Napoleon is quoted as saying, **"is a word found only in the dictionary of fools."**

It's smart to pick your friends... but not to pieces.

☆ ☆ ☆ ☆ ☆

LIFE'S MIRROR

There are loyal hearts, there are spirits brave, there are souls that are pure and true; then give to the world the best you have, and the best will come back to you.

Give love, and love to your life will flow, a strength in your utmost need; have faith, and a score of hearts will show their faith in your word and deed.

Give truth, and your gift will be paid in kind, and honor will honor meet; and a smile that is sweet will surely find a smile that is just as sweet.

Give sorrow and pity to those who mourn; you will gather in flowers again the scattered seeds of your thought outbourne, though the sowing seemed but vain.

For life is the mirror of king and slave 'tis just what we are and do; then give to the world the best you have, just the best will come back to you.

Madeline S. Bridges

☆ ☆ ☆ ☆ ☆

YOU'RE GETTING OLD WHEN YOU REACH THE METALLIC AGE: YOUR TEETH ARE GOLD, YOUR HAIR SILVER, AND YOU HAVE LEAD IN YOUR PANTS.

"The woods are lovely, dark and deep,
But I have promises to keep,
And miles to go before I sleep,
And miles to go before I sleep."
Robert Frost

☆ ☆ ☆ ☆ ☆

MAN'S NEED

Just to need to be needed by someone is the whole of man's mission on Earth.

It's the total, the sum of his purpose, it's the ultimate goal of his worth.

In a world that is wanting in freedom, in a nation with pockets of poor, in a city with problems aplenty, there is need for man's goal - to be sure.

There is need on the busiest homefront.

There is need where it's quiet and alone.

He who finds him a spot where he's needed fills the paramount need of his own.

Margaret Rorke

☆ ☆ ☆ ☆ ☆

Men give me some credit for genius. All the genius I have lies in this: When I have a subject in hand, I study it profoundly. Day and night it is before me. I explore it in all its bearings. My mind becomes pervaded with it. Then the efforts that I make are what people are pleased to call the fruits of genius. It is the fruit of labor and thought! **Alexander Hamilton**

IF YOU HAD A FRIEND

If you had a friend strong, simple, true, who knew your faults and who understood; who believed in the very best of you, and who cared fore you as a father would; who would stick by you to the very end, who would smile however the world might frown: I'm sure you would try to please your friend, you never would think to throw him down.

And supposing your friend was high and great, and he lived in a palace rich and tall, and sat like a King in shining state, and his praise was loud on the lips of all; well then, when he turned to you alone, and singled you out from all the crowd, and he called you up to his golden throne, oh , wouldn't you just be jolly proud?

If you had a friend like this , I say, so sweet and tender, so strong and true, you'd live at your bravest - now, wouldn't you? His worth would shine in the words you penned; you'd shout his praises... yet now it's odd! You tell me you haven't got such a friend; you haven't? I wonder... *What of God?*

-Robert Service

☆ ☆ ☆ ☆ ☆

Nobody can make a fool out of a person if he isn't the right kind of material for the job.

The difference between good and great is just a little extra effort.
Duffy Daugherty

☆ ☆ ☆ ☆ ☆

IN A FRIENDLY SORT OF WAY
By James W. Riley

When a man ain't got a cent and he's feeling kind of blue, and the clouds hang dark and heavy and won't let the sunshine through, it's a great thing, oh, my brethren, for a fellow just to lay his hand upon your shoulder in a friendly sort o'way.

It makes a man feel curious, it makes the teardrops start, an you sort o'feel a flutter in the region of your heart. You can't look up and meet his eyes, you just don't know what to say, when a hand is on your shoulder in a friendly sort o'way.

Oh, the world's a curious compound, with its honey and its gall, with its cares and bitter crosses, but a good world after all. And a good God must have made it, leastwise that is what I say, when a hand is on my shoulder in a friendly sort o'way.

☆ ☆ ☆ ☆ ☆

FAILURE IS THE LINE OF LEAST PERSISTENCE.
— W.A. CLARK

An executive is a man employed to talk with visitors so that the other employees can keep on working.

☆ ☆ ☆ ☆ ☆

BE

Be understanding to your enemies.
Be loyal to your friends.
Be strong enough to face the world each day.
Be weak enough to know you cannot do everything alone.
Be generous to those who need help.
Be frugal with what you need yourself.
Be wise enough to know that you do not know everything.
Be foolish enough to believe in miracles.
Be willing to share your joys.
Be willing to share the sorrow of others.
Be a leader when you see a path others have missed.
Be a follower when you are shrouded by the mists of uncertainty.
Be the first to congratulate an opponent who succeeds.
Be the last to criticize a colleague who fails.
Be sure where your next step will fall so that you will not stumble.
Be sure of your final destination, in case you are going the wrong way.
Be loving to those who love you.

☆ ☆ ☆ ☆ ☆

I NEVER KNEW A MAN WHO WAS GOOD AT MAKING EXCUSES WHO WAS GOOD AT ANYTHING ELSE.   BEN FRANKLIN

We are what we repeatedly do. Excellence, then, is not an **act** but a **habit**.   **Aristotle**

☆ ☆ ☆ ☆

COMFORT
by Robert Service

Say! You've struck a heap of trouble—
Bust in business, lost your wife;
No one cares a cent about you,
You don't care a cent for life;
Hard luck has of hope bereft you,
Health is failing, wish you'd die—
Why, you've still the sunshine left you
And the big, blue sky.

Sky so blue it makes you wonder
If it's heaven shining through;
Earth so smiling 'way out yonder,
Sun so bright it dazzles you;
Birds a-singing, flowers a-flinging
All their fragrance on the breeze;
Dancing shadows, green, still meadows—
Don't you mope, you've still got these.

These, and none can take them from you;
These, and none can weigh their worth.
What? You're tired and broke and beaten?
Why, you're rich—you've got the earth!
Yes, if you're a tramp in tatters,
While the blue sky bends above;
You've got nearly all that matters,
You've got God, and God is love.

☆ ☆ ☆ ☆

It wouldn't be so bad to let one's mind go blank if one always remembered to turn off the sound...

There is a relationship — an almost uncanny relationship — which exists between a man's income and his ability to use his language. Words are tools, and the more tools we have, the more jobs we can handle.
Earl Nightingale

☆ ☆ ☆ ☆

WHEN THINGS GO WRONG

I count it best, when things go wrong, to hum a tune and sing a song; a heavy heart means sure defeat, but joy is victory replete.

If skies are cloudy, count the gain. New life depends upon the rain; the cuckoo carols loud and long when clouds hang low and things go wrong.

When things go wrong, remember then the happy heart has strength of ten; forget the sorrow, sing a song — it makes all right when things go wrong.
Charles Henry Chelsey

☆ ☆ ☆ ☆

Five rules for job failure:
1) Do only what is required.
2) Leave it to the last minute.
3) Let the mistakes go.
4) Don't listen to your conscience.
5) Learn to be a convincing bluffer.

☆ ☆ ☆ ☆

He who is afraid of doing too much always does too little.

The man who is bigger than his job keeps cool. He does not lose his head, he refuses to become rattled, to fly off in a temper. The man who would control others must be able to control himself. There is something admirable, something inspiring, something soul-stirring about a man who displays coolness and courage under extremely trying circumstances. A good temper is not only a business asset. It is the secret of health. The longer you live, the more you will learn that a disordered temper breeds a disordered body.
B.C. Forbes

☆ ☆ ☆ ☆ ☆

Better a day of strife than a century of sleep.

☆ ☆ ☆ ☆ ☆

Play Boldly?

If you're going to play boldly, the reality is that you've got to expect trouble and know how to get out of it. Ninety percent of the time you can do it, *if* you know how, and have the discipline to try. For scrambling out of trouble isn't a matter of compounding error with recklessness in the "miracle of the mind", it's a matter of developing an awareness of reality that can expand your horizons instead of contracting them with fear or apprehension, or even with a resigned sense of defeat.
-Arnold Palmer

"The future does not belong to those who are content with today, apathetic toward common problems and their fellow man alike, timid and fearful in the face of new ideas and bold projects. Rather it will belong to those who can blend vision, reason and courage in a personal commitment to the ideals and great enterprises of American society."
Bobby Kennedy

☆ ☆ ☆ ☆ ☆

SOME PEOPLE ARE CONFIDENT THEY COULD MOVE MOUNTAINS IF ONLY SOMEBODY WOULD JUST CLEAR THE FOOTHILLS OUT OF THE WAY.

☆ ☆ ☆ ☆ ☆

Our future may live beyond our vision, but is not completely beyond our control. The shaping impulse of America is that neither fate, nor nature, nor the irresistible tides of history, but the work of our own hands, matched to reason and principle, determines our destiny. There is pride in that, even arrogance, but there is also experience and truth. In any event, it is the only way we can live.

☆ ☆ ☆ ☆ ☆

Success without honor is an unseasoned dish: it will satisfy your hunger, but it won't taste good.
Joe Paterno

WINNERS vs. LOSERS

The **Winner** is always a part of the answer
The **Loser** is always a part of the problem

The **Winner** always has a program
The **Loser** always has an excuse

The **Winner** says "Let me do it for you"
The **Loser** says "That's not my job"

The **Winner** sees an answer for every problem
The **Loser** sees problems in every answer

The **Winner** sees a green near every sand trap
The **Loser** sees two or three sand traps near every green

The **Winner** says: "It may be difficult, but it's possible"
The **Loser** says: "It may be possible, but it's too difficult"

BE A WINNER!

☆ ☆ ☆ ☆

A young man entered an office in response to a sign "Boy Wanted". "What kind of boy do you want?" he asked the manager. "Why, we want a clean, well-groomed, neat youngster," replied the manager, "who is quiet, quick, and obedient." "Phooey!" said the youth disgustedly, turning to leave. "You don't want a boy, you want a girl!"

☆ ☆ ☆ ☆

HONOR IS ALWAYS BETTER THAN HONORS.

GRIN
by Robert Service

If you're up against a bruiser and you're getting knocked about -- **Grin**.
If you're feeling pretty groggy, and you're licked beyond a doubt -- **Grin**.
Don't let him see you're funking, let him know with every clout, though your face is battered to a pulp, your blooming heart is stout; just stand upon your pins until the beggar knocks you out -- and **grin**. This life's a bully battle, and the same advice holds true of **grin**. If you're up against it badly, then it's only one on you, so **grin**. If the future's black as thunder, don't let people see you're blue; just cultivate a cast-iron smile of joy the whole day through. If they call you "Little Sunshine," wish that they'd no troubles, too -- you may -- **grin**.
Rise up in the morning with the will that, smooth or rough, you'll **grin**.
Sink to sleep at midnight and although you're feeling tough, yet **grin**.
There's nothing gained by whining, and you're not that kind of stuff; you're a fighter from away back, and you won't take a rebuff; your trouble is that you don't know when you have had enough - don't give in.
If Fate should down you, just get up and take another cuff; you may bank on it that there is no philosophy like bluff, and **grin**.

41

Great ideas need landing gears as well as wings.

☆ ☆ ☆ ☆ ☆

To Dad on Father's Day 1977
From Jill and Jenny
Happiness is possible only when one is busy. The body must toil, the mind must be occupied, and the heart must be satisfied. Those who do good as opportunity offers are sowing seed all the time, and they need not doubt the harvest.

☆ ☆ ☆ ☆ ☆

EVEN THE BEST IDEAS WILL RARELY WORK UNLESS YOU DO.

☆ ☆ ☆ ☆ ☆

Nothing is easier than fault-finding: No brains & no character are required to set up in the grumbling business.

☆ ☆ ☆ ☆ ☆

Good executives thrive on problems because it is their job to solve them calmly and efficiently.
Guy Ferguson

The best way to make an impression is by making the impression that you're not trying to make an impression.
G. Hart

☆ ☆ ☆ ☆ ☆

The characteristic of heroism is its persistency. All men have wandering impulses, fits and starts of generosity. But when you have chosen your part, abide by it, and do not weakly try to reconcile yourself with the world. The heroic cannot be the common, nor the common the heroic. Yet we have the weakness to expect the sympathy of people in those actions whose excellence is that they outrun sympathy and appeal to a tardy justice. If you would serve your brother, because it is fit for you to serve him, do not take back your words when you find that prudent people do not commend you. Adhere to your own act and congratulate yourself if you have done something strange and extravagant and broken the monotony of a decorous age. It was a high counsel that I once heard given to a young person: **"Always do what you are afraid to do."** Ralph Waldo Emerson

☆ ☆ ☆ ☆ ☆

ONE OF THE MOST FREQUENT CAUSES FOR FAILURE OF ABLE-BODIED MEN IS IMPATIENCE IN WAITING FOR RESULTS.

☆ ☆ ☆ ☆ ☆

The hardest thing about life is that it's so daily.

I can see how it might be possible for a man to look down upon the earth and be an atheist, but I cannot conceive how he could look up into the heavens and say there is no God.

      Abraham Lincoln

☆ ☆ ☆ ☆ ☆

"Some believe there is nothing one man or one woman can do against the enormous array of the world's ills. Yet many of the world's great movements, of thought and action, have flowed from the work of a single man. A young monk began the Protestant Reformation, a young general extended an empire from Macedonia to the borders of the earth, and a young woman reclaimed the territory of France. It was a young Italian explorer who discovered the New World, and thirty-two-year-old Thomas Jefferson who proclaimed that all men are created equal."

      Robert F. Kennedy

☆ ☆ ☆ ☆

DO MORE

Do more than exist - *live*
Do more than touch - *feel*
Do more than look - *observe*
Do more than read - *absorb*
Do more than hear - *listen*
Do more than listen - *understand*
Do more than think - *ponder*
Do more than plan - *act*
Do more than talk - *say something*

THINK LIKE A WINNER

What are the traits that make one man a winner and another man a loser? The big difference is in how a man thinks. His attitude will govern his actions. For instance:

A winner is always ready to tackle something new. A loser is prone to believe it can't be done.
A winner isn't afraid of competition. A loser excuses himself with the idea that the competition beat him out.
A winner knows he's sometimes wrong and is willing to admit his mistakes. A loser can usually find someone to blame.
A winner is challenged by a new problem. A loser doesn't want to face it.
A winner is decisive. A loser frustrates himself with indecision.
A winner realizes there is no time like the present to get a job done. A loser is prone to procrastinate with the hope that things will be better tomorrow.
A winner thinks positively, acts positively and lives positively. A loser usually has a negative approach to everything.

So, if **you** want to be a winner, *think* like a winner, *act* like a winner, and, sooner than you think, **you** will *be* a winner.

☆ ☆ ☆ ☆ ☆

THE GREATEST MISTAKE A MAN CAN MAKE IS TO SACRIFICE HEALTH FOR ANY OTHER ADVANTAGE.

Andrew Carnegie:
"As I grow older, I pay less attention to what men say. I just watch what they do."

☆ ☆ ☆ ☆ ☆

ANYWAY

People are unreasonable, illogical and self centered. Love them anyway.
If you do good, people will accuse you of selfish motives. Do good anyway.
If you are successful you will win false friends and true enemies. Succeed anyway.
The good you do today will be forgotten tomorrow. Do good anyway.
Honesty and frankness make you vulnerable. Be honest and frank anyway.
People favor underdogs but follow only top dogs. Fight for some underdogs anyway.
What you spend years building may be destroyed overnight. Build anyway.
People really need help but may attack you if you help them. Help people anyway.
Give the world the best you have and you'll get kicked in the teeth.
Give the world the best you've got...
                    ANYWAY.

☆ ☆ ☆ ☆ ☆

Middle management, it is said, is the level where you still hear the rumors, but you're not high enough to know if they're true.

IF YOU EVER FIND A MAN WHO IS BETTER THAN YOU ARE—HIRE HIM. IF NECESSARY, PAY HIM MORE THAN YOU PAY YOURSELF.
DAVID OGILVY

☆ ☆ ☆ ☆ ☆

THE SONG OF THE WAGE-SLAVE
by Robert Service

Never knew kiss of sweetheart, never caress of wife. A brute with brute strength to labor, and they were so far above—yet I'd gladly have gone to the gallows for one little look of Love.

I, with the strength of two men, savage and shy and wild—yet how I'd ha' treasured a woman, and the sweet, warm kiss of a child! Well, 'tis Thy world, and Thou knowest. I blaspheme and my ways be rude; but I've lived my life as I found it, and I've done my best to be good; I, the primitive toiler, half naked and grimed to the eyes, sweating it deep in their ditches, swining it stark in their sties; hurling down forests before me, spanning tumultuous streams; down in the ditch building o'er me palaces fairer than dreams; boring the rock to the ore-bed, driving the road through the fen; resolute, dumb, uncomplaining, a man in a world of men. Master, I've filled my contract, wrought in Thy many lands, not by my sins wilt Thou judge me, but by the work of my hands. Master, I've done Thy bidding, and the light is low in the west, and the long, long shift is over...Master, I've earned it--rest.

HOW DO WE MEASURE A MAN?

What can we use when we measure a man? What can we use for the test? It isn't a yardstick, it isn't a scale, for size doesn't make him the best.
It isn't the kind of job that he holds, nor the money he has in the bank, nor his college degrees, nor the clothes that he wears, nor his titles, position, nor rank.

The measure that counts, that makes him a *man*, is the way that he wears with his friends; it's the kindness he shows, the pleasures he shares and the unselfish service he lends.

It's his everyday living, the interest he takes, in his day-by-day dealings with others; his desire to help, his love of mankind, that sets him apart from his brothers.

He doesn't seek honors, he doesn't seek fame. His friendliness isn't a plan; just the way that he lives, passes all of the tests, that we use when we measure a *man*.

John Waters

☆ ☆ ☆ ☆ ☆

Life is like a taxi. The meter just keeps a-ticking whether you are getting somewhere or just standing still.
Lou Erickson

☆ ☆ ☆ ☆ ☆

Lord give me patience...
and I want it right now!

LIFE ISN'T LIKE A BOOK. LIFE ISN'T LOGICAL OR SENSIBLE OR ORDERLY. LIFE IS A MESS MOST OF THE TIME. AND THEOLOGY MUST BE LIVED IN THE MIDST OF THAT MESS.
CHARLES COLSON

☆ ☆ ☆ ☆ ☆

WHAT IS LIFE?
Life is a challenge - *meet it*
Life is a gift - *accept it*
Life is an adventure - *dare it*
Life is a sorrow - *overcome it*
Life is a tragedy - *face it*
Life is a duty - *perform it*
Life is a game - *play it*
Life is a mystery - *unfold it*
Life is a song - *sing it*
Life is an opportunity - *take it*
Life is a journey - *complete it*
Life is a promise - *fulfill it*
Life is a beauty - *praise it*
Life is a struggle - *fight it*
Life is a goal - *achieve it*
Life is a puzzle - *solve it*

☆ ☆ ☆ ☆ ☆

We must have sympathy for the loser. We must help the poor. But, let us also cheer for the doer, the Achiever.   VINCE LOMBARDI

☆ ☆ ☆ ☆ ☆

So much of what we call management consists in making it difficult for people to work.
Peter Drucker

A good manager is a man who isn't worried about his own career, but rather, the careers of those who work for him. Take care of those who work for you and you'll float to greatness on their achievements.

H.S.M. Burns

☆ ☆ ☆ ☆ ☆

Are you playing the game on the field of life? Are you keeping within the rules?

Do you play with a jump and a joy in the strife, nor whimper for better tools?

There is always a chap who lags behind, and wails that the world is gray;

That his ax is dull, and his wheel won't grind, and it's too late to begin today.

But if you should ask the other chap, the one who has gone ahead, you'll find that his tolls were worse, mayhap; and he's made new ones instead.

For playing the game means not to grin, when the field is smooth and clear;

But to fight from the first for the joy therein, nor to heed the haunt of fear.

And though in the strife no prize you earn that marks the victor's fame;

Know still, if you've tried at every turn, you have won, for you've played the game!

Raymond Comstock

Thomas Jefferson's Philosophy

In matters of principle, stand like a rock, in matters of taste, swim with the current. Give up money, give up fame, give up science, give up the earth itself and all it contains, rather than do an immoral act. And never suppose that in any possible situation, or under any circumstances, it is best for you to do a dishonorable thing, though it can never be known but to appear to you. Whenever you are to do a thing, though it can never be known but to yourself, ask yourself how you would act were all the world looking at you, and act accordingly. He who permits himself to tell a lie once, finds it much easier to do it a second and third time, 'till at length it becomes habitual; he tells a lie without attending to it, and truths without the world's believing him.

☆ ☆ ☆ ☆ ☆

It is more important to know where you are going than to get there quickly. Do not mistake activity for achievement.
Mabel Newcomer

☆ ☆ ☆ ☆ ☆

Remember this your lifetime through —
Tomorrow, there will be more to do and failure waits for all who stay with some success made yesterday.
Tomorrow, you must try once more and even harder than before.

Actually, there are only four primary sales appeals to persuade others to action. **They are The Four S's:**

Sex...to make a favorable impression on the other sex
Snob...to keep up with the Joneses
Self...to improve one's status in life
Soul...to be at peace with God.

☆ ☆ ☆ ☆ ☆

NINE RULES FOR SUCCESS

1. Learn to get along with people. Make people like you.
2. Learn to exhibit more patience than any other person you know.
3. Respect other men's and women's opinions and ideas.
4. Learn to think problems through. Don't give up. If you don't get the answer today, go back at it tomorrow. Discipline your mind to the thought that anything given you to decide, presupposes your ability to solve it. Sufficient thought will bring the proper solution in due time.
5. Learn to put yourself in the other fellow's place. There are two sides to every dispute, and yours is not necessarily the right one. Keep an open mind, no matter how personal the point at issue.
6. Be humble.
7. Be loyal.
8. Cultivate cheerfulness.
9. Work

HE WHO CANNOT FORGIVE, DESTROYS THE BRIDGE OVER WHICH HE MAY ONE DAY NEED TO PASS.

☆ ☆ ☆ ☆ ☆

MYSELF

I have to live with myself, and so I want to be fit for myself to know I want to be able, as days go by, always to look myself straight in the eye; I don't want to stand, with the setting sun, and hate myself for things I have done.

I don't want to keep on a closet shelf a lot of secrets about myself, and fool myself, as I come and go, into thinking that nobody else will know the kind of a man I really am; I don't want to dress up myself in shame.

I want to go out with my head erect, I want to deserve all men's respect; but here in the struggle for fame and wealth I want to be able to like myself. I don't want to look at myself and know that I'm bluster and bluff and empty show.

I can never hide myself from me; I see what others may never see; I know what others may never know, I never can fool myself, and so, whatever happens, I want to be self-respecting and conscience free.

Edgar A. Guest

☆ ☆ ☆ ☆ ☆

Don't look for an answer to your problem; look for *lots* of answers, then choose the best one.

> **Life is an uphill battle for the guy who's not on the level.**
> — Joan Welsh

☆ ☆ ☆ ☆ ☆

YOU TELL ON YOURSELF

You tell what you are by the friends you seek, by the very manner in which you speak, by the way you employ your leisure time, by the use you make of the dollar and dime.

You tell what you are by the things you wear, by the spirit in which your burdens bear, by the kinds of things at which you laugh, by the records you play on your phonograph.

You tell what you are by the way you walk, by the things of which delight you to talk, by the manner in which you bear defeat, by so simple a thing as how you eat. By the books you choose from the well-filled shelf, in these ways and more, you tell on yourself. So, there's really no particular sense in any effort at false pretense.

☆ ☆ ☆ ☆ ☆

LIFE IS A GRINDSTONE. WHETHER IT GRINDS A MAN DOWN OR POLISHES HIM DEPENDS UPON THE KIND OF STUFF HE IS MADE OF.

☆ ☆ ☆ ☆ ☆

CHARACTER...
IS WHAT A MAN IS IN THE DARK

**Every evening I turn worries over to God.
He's going to be up all night anyway.**
        Mary C. Crowley

☆ ☆ ☆ ☆ ☆

YOUR NAME

You got it from your father
It was all he had to give
So it's yours to use and cherish
For as long as you may live.
If you lose the watch he gave you,
It can always be replaced
But a black mark on your name,
Son, Can never be erased.
It was clean the day you took it.
And a worthy name to bear
When he got it from his father,
There was no dishonor there.
So make sure you guard it wisely,
After all is said and done
You'll be glad the name is spotless
When you give it to your son.

☆ ☆ ☆ ☆ ☆

THE HUMAN SPIRIT IS STRONGER THAN ANYTHING THAT CAN HAPPEN TO IT.
        C.C. Scott

☆ ☆ ☆ ☆ ☆

**Every accomplishment great or small...
starts with the decision
I'll Try!**

Are you trying to make something for yourself or something of yourself?

☆ ☆ ☆ ☆ ☆

IT CAN BE DONE

Somebody said that it couldn't be done, but he with a chuckle replied, that "maybe it couldn't" but he would be one who wouldn't say so 'till he'd tried. So he buckled right in with a trace of a grin on his face. If he worried, he hid it. He started to sing as he tackled the thing that couldn't be done. And he did it.

Somebody scoffed "Oh, you'll never do that, at least no one ever has done it." But he took off his coat and took off his hat and the first thing he knew he'd begun it. With the lift of his chin and a bit of a grin, if any doubt rose he forbid it; he started to sing as he tackled the thing that couldn't be done, and he did it.

There are thousands to tell you it cannot be done, there are thousands to prophesy failure; there are thousands to point out to you, one by one, the dangers that wait to assail you. But just buckle right in with a bit of a grin, then take off your coat and go to it. Just start in to sing as you tackle the thing that cannot be done, and you'll do it.

☆ ☆ ☆ ☆ ☆

The statistics on death are quite impressive. 100 people out of every 100 people will die.

THE GREATEST THINGS

THE GREATEST PUZZLE - **Life**
THE GREATEST THOUGHT - **God**
THE BEST WORK - **Work you like**
THE GREATEST MISTAKE - **Giving up**
THE MOST RIDICULOUS ASSET - **Pride**
THE GREATEST NEED - **Common sense**
THE MOST DANGEROUS PERSON - **A liar**
THE MOST EXPENSIVE INDULGENCE - **Hate**
THE MOST DISAGREEABLE PERSON - **The complainer**
THE BEST TEACHER - **One who makes you want to learn**
THE GREATEST DECEIVER - **The one who deceives himself**
THE WORST BANKRUPT - **The soul who has lost enthusiasm**
THE CHEAPEST, EASIEST, AND MOST STUPID THING TO DO - **Finding fault**
THE CLEVEREST MAN - **The one who always does what he thinks is right**
THE GREATEST COMFORT - **The knowledge that you have done your work well**
THE MEANEST FEELING OF WHICH ANY HUMAN IS CAPABLE - **Feeling envious of another's success**
THE GREATEST THING- BAR NONE - IN THE WORLD **Love. Love for family, home, friends, neighbors and for the land in which we enjoy our freedom.**

☆ ☆ ☆ ☆

You can tell more about a person by what he says about others than you can by what others say about him.

> "It's what you learn after you know it all that counts."
> John Wooden
> UCLA Basketball

☆ ☆ ☆ ☆ ☆

"You know, whether it's in business, politics, education, or athletics, there has to be respect and loyalty for the leader. Success or failure depends on it. There are three questions from the leader that must be answered affirmatively by individual group members if the group needs assurance that it can reach its desired goal. Can I trust you? Are you committed? Do you respect or care about me? If the individuals can answer "yes" to their leader to these three questions, even greatness is within their grasp."
Lou Holtz

☆ ☆ ☆ ☆ ☆

Decision is a sharp knife that cuts clean and straight; indecision is a dull one that hacks and tears and leaves ragged edges behind it.
Gordon Graham

☆ ☆ ☆ ☆ ☆

A boss cannot <u>make</u> you do anything, but he can surely make you regret you didn't.

It matters not where you are today, but in what direction you are moving and where you will finish.

☆ ☆ ☆ ☆ ☆

TIME

Few people actually waste time - they misuse it. Misusing time means not delegating work, not scheduling days, not making decisions, not establishing priorities.

Effective, successful people are people who get maximum benefit from a minimum investment of time. They are aware that time is their greatest asset and that it must be used with the utmost discretion.

☆ ☆ ☆ ☆ ☆

One of the qualities I would certainly look for in an executive is whether he knows how to delegate properly. The inability to do this is, in my opinion (and in that of others I have talked with on this subject), one of the chief reasons executives fail. Another is their inability to make decisions effectively. These two personality lacks have contributed more to executive failure than any amount of know-how lacks.   J.C. Penney

☆ ☆ ☆ ☆ ☆

Life is being, not having.

MANY OF LIFE'S FAILURES ARE MEN WHO DID NOT REALIZE HOW CLOSE THEY WERE TO SUCCESS WHEN THEY GAVE UP.

☆ ☆ ☆ ☆ ☆

Economics is extremely useful as a form of employment for economists.

☆ ☆ ☆ ☆ ☆

It's a funny thing about life: if you refuse to accept anything but the very best you will very often get it.
W. Somerset Maugham

☆ ☆ ☆ ☆ ☆

If better is possible, good is not enough.

☆ ☆ ☆ ☆ ☆

IT'S HELL TO WORK FOR A NERVOUS BOSS, ESPECIALLY WHEN YOU ARE THE ONE WHO IS MAKING HIM NERVOUS.

☆ ☆ ☆ ☆ ☆

Swallowing angry words is much easier than having to eat them.

ARE YOU WORKING TOO HARD?

Who isn't working too hard? Run through our tongue-in-cheek checklist below. If more than five of the points apply to you, maybe you are working too hard!

1. You rush home from your 9-to-5 job just in time to catch the 11 o'clock news.

2. You wake up at 7 A.M. and get dressed for work before you realize it's Saturday.

3. You answer your home phone "Acme Widget Company".

4. You eat breakfast, lunch and dinner at the office.

5. You wake up from a nightmare in which the copy machine is chasing you.

6. You buy more new underwear because you haven't had a chance to do your laundry.

7. You look forward to the weekends so you can catch up on work when the office is quiet.

8. You type your food-shopping list.

9. You keep an in/out box on your dresser.

10. Your dog doesn't recognize you.

11. You're on a first-name basis with all the night watchmen.

12. More of your personal belongings are at work than at home—dishes, shoes, plants, photos.

13. You have no time to look for a new job.

A DAY OFF...

So you want the day off? Let's take a look at what you are asking for:

There are **365** days per year available for work. There are **52** weeks per year in which you already have **2** days off per week, leaving **261** days available for work. Since you spend **16** hours each day away from work, you have used up **170** days, leaving only **91** days available. You spend **30** minutes each day on coffee break. That accounts for **23** days each year, leaving only **68** days available. With a one-hour lunch period each day, you have used up another **48** days, leaving only **22** days available for work. You normally spend **2** days per year on sick leave. This leaves you only **20** days available for work. We offer **5** holidays per year, so your available working time is down to **15** days. We generously give you **14** days vacation per year which leaves you only **1** day available for work, and I'll be damned if you're going to take that day off!!!

☆ ☆ ☆ ☆ ☆

THAT'S NOT MY JOB...

This is a story about four people named **Everybody**, **Anybody**, **Somebody** and **Nobody**.

There was an important job to be done and **Everybody** was sure that **Somebody** would do it. **Anybody** could have done it, but **Nobody** did it. **Somebody** got angry about that because it was **Everybody's** job. **Everybody** thought **Anybody** could do it, but **Nobody** realized that **Everybody** wouldn't do it. It ended up that **Everybody** blamed **Somebody** when **Nobody** did what **Anybody** could have done.

THE SECRETARY'S PRAYER

Dear Lord, I need help. Help me to be a good subordinate and help me to have the memory of an elephant, or one at least three years long. Help me by some miracle to be able to do six things at once, answer four telephones at the same time while typing a letter that must go out today. And, when that letter doesn't get signed until tomorrow, give me the strength to keep from going over the brink of hysteria. Never let me lose patience, even when the boss has me searching the files for hours for data that is later discovered in his desk.

Help me to have the intelligence of a college professor; help me to understand and carry out all instructions without any explanation. Let me know always just where the boss is, what he's doing, and when he will be back, even though he did leave without telling me where he was going. And when the year ends, please let me have the foresight not to destroy records that will be asked for in a few days, even though I have been told to destroy them.

Help me to keep a level head and my feet on the ground, so that my secretarial performance will be a proper reflection of the pioneer women who made a place for me in the business world, and those who established me in a profession.

☆ ☆ ☆ ☆

No person can ever be happy until he has learned to enjoy what he has and not to worry over what he does not have.

ENTHUSIASM IN YOUR WORK IS HALF THE BATTLE WON.

☆ ☆ ☆ ☆

What Is Hustle?

Hustle is doing something that everyone is absolutely certain can't be done.

Hustle is getting the order because you got there first, or stayed with it after everyone else gave up.

Hustle is shoe leather and elbow grease and sweat and missing lunch.

Hustle is getting prospects to say "yes" after they've said "no" twenty times.

Hustle is doing more unto a customer than the other guy is doing unto him.

Hustle is believing in yourself and the business you're in.

Hustle is the sheer joy of winning.

Hustle is being the sorest loser in town.

Hustle is hating to take a vacation because you might miss a piece of the action.

Hustle is heaven if you're a hustler.

Hustle is hell if you're not.

☆ ☆ ☆ ☆ ☆

The dictionary is the only place *success* comes before *work*.

☆ ☆ ☆ ☆ ☆

Life is a lot like tennis: the one who can serve best seldom loses.

If you don't get everything you want, think of the things you don't get that you don't want.

☆ ☆ ☆ ☆ ☆

The In's and Out's of Your Job

It's **IN** to care about your job; it's **OUT** to bite the hand that feeds you.
It's **IN** to be loyal to the company that pays you; it's **OUT** to breed discontent.
It's **IN** to give a little more than expected; it's **OUT** to split when you haven't finished the task at hand. It's **IN** to be courteous - to anticipate the needs of fellow employees and plan accordingly; it's **OUT** to operate on your own, disregarding your obligation to others.
It's **IN** to appreciate all the benefits we enjoy; it's **OUT** to take all the benefits without making the best of what remains
 It's **IN** to praise fellow workers, while they're alive to hear it; it's **OUT** to wait until their wakes to say something nice.
It's **IN** to communicate with each other; it's **OUT** to withhold what is necessary to operate a business. It's **IN** to contribute, to get involved, to remain active; it's **OUT** to be passive, and pessimistic and aloof.
It's **IN** to work and win; it's **OUT** to exist and lose.
It's **IN** to make productive the days that will never come back; it's **OUT** to let the days drift by and wonder why you died of boredom.
It's **IN** to love your job; it's **OUT** to endure it.

By Mary Sweeney

**If you can imagine it, you can achieve it.
If you can dream it, you can become it.**

☆ ☆ ☆ ☆ ☆

The Garden of Life

First, plant five rows of **P's**:
    Presence
    Promptness
    Preparation
    Perseverance
    Purity

Next, plant three rows of **squash**:
    Squash gossip
    Squash indifference
    Squash unjust criticism

Then plant five rows of **lettuce:**
    Let us be faithful to duty
    Let us be unselfish and loyal
    Let us obey the rules and regulations
    Let us be true to our obligations
    Let us love one another

No garden is complete without **turnups:**
    Turn up for meetings
    Turn up with a smile
    Turn up with determination to make everything count for something good and worthwhile.

☆ ☆ ☆ ☆ ☆

**SUCCESS IS GETTING WHAT YOU WANT,
HAPPINESS IS WANTING WHAT YOU GET.**

Every evening I turn worries over to God.
He's going to be up all night anyway.
                  Mary C. Crowley

☆ ☆ ☆ ☆ ☆

YOUR NAME

You got it from your father
It was all he had to give
So it's yours to use and cherish
For as long as you may live.
If you lose the watch he gave you,
It can always be replaced
But a black mark on your name,
Son, Can never be erased.
It was clean the day you took it.
And a worthy name to bear
When he got it from his father,
There was no dishonor there.
So make sure you guard it wisely,
After all is said and done
You'll be glad the name is spotless
When you give it to your son.

☆ ☆ ☆ ☆ ☆

THE HUMAN SPIRIT IS STRONGER THAN ANYTHING THAT CAN HAPPEN TO IT.
                  C.C. Scott

☆ ☆ ☆ ☆ ☆

Every accomplishment great or small...
starts with the decision
I'll Try!

Are you trying to make something for yourself or something of yourself?

☆ ☆ ☆ ☆ ☆

IT CAN BE DONE

Somebody said that it couldn't be done, but he with a chuckle replied, that "maybe it couldn't" but he would be one who wouldn't say so 'till he'd tried. So he buckled right in with a trace of a grin on his face. If he worried, he hid it. He started to sing as he tackled the thing that couldn't be done. And he did it.

Somebody scoffed "Oh, you'll never do that, at least no one ever has done it." But he took off his coat and took off his hat and the first thing he knew he'd begun it. With the lift of his chin and a bit of a grin, if any doubt rose he forbid it; he started to sing as he tackled the thing that couldn't be done, and he did it.

There are thousands to tell you it cannot be done, there are thousands to prophesy failure; there are thousands to point out to you, one by one, the dangers that wait to assail you. But just buckle right in with a bit of a grin, then take off your coat and go to it. Just start in to sing as you tackle the thing that cannot be done, and you'll do it.

☆ ☆ ☆ ☆ ☆

The statistics on death are quite impressive. 100 people out of every 100 people will die.

NO PRICE IS TOO HIGH TO PAY FOR A GOOD REPUTATION.

☆ ☆ ☆ ☆

Promise Yourself —
To be strong, that nothing can disturb your peace of mind.
To talk health, happiness, and prosperity to every person you meet.
To make your friends feel that there is something in them.
To look at the sunny side of everything and make your optimism come true.
To think only of the best, to work only for the best and to expect only the best.
To be just as enthusiastic about the success of others as you are about your own.
To forget the mistakes of the past and press on to the greater achievements of the future.
To wear a cheerful countenance at all times and give every living creature you meet a smile.
To give so much time to the improvement of yourself that you have no time to criticize others.
To be too large for worry, too noble for anger, too strong for fear, and too happy to permit the presence of trouble.

Christian D. Larson

☆ ☆ ☆ ☆

To activate others, to get them to be enthusiastic, you must first be enthusiastic yourself.

Mankind is divided into three classes:
>Those who are immoveable,
>>Those who are moveable,
>>>And those who **move**.

☆ ☆ ☆ ☆ ☆

"Your bosses, peers and subordinates are influenced not by your competence but by their confidence in your competence; not by your personality but by their rapport with your personality; not by your character but by their respect for your character. These acquired influences have to be continuously cultivated by management and stimulated for repetition among subordinates."

This is the judgment of **William Oncken Jr.**, as expressed in "*Managing Management Time: Who's Got the Money?*"

☆ ☆ ☆ ☆ ☆

NOT TO DECIDE IS TO DECIDE.
>Harvey Cox

☆ ☆ ☆ ☆ ☆

The difference between education and experience: Education is what you get from reading the small print. Experience is what you get from not reading it.

THE GREATEST THINGS

THE GREATEST PUZZLE - **Life**
THE GREATEST THOUGHT - **God**
THE BEST WORK - **Work you like**
THE GREATEST MISTAKE - **Giving up**
THE MOST RIDICULOUS ASSET - **Pride**
THE GREATEST NEED - **Common sense**
THE MOST DANGEROUS PERSON - **A liar**
THE MOST EXPENSIVE INDULGENCE - **Hate**
THE MOST DISAGREEABLE PERSON - **The complainer**
THE BEST TEACHER - **One who makes you want to learn**
THE GREATEST DECEIVER - **The one who deceives himself**
THE WORST BANKRUPT - **The soul who has lost enthusiasm**
THE CHEAPEST, EASIEST, AND MOST STUPID THING TO DO - **Finding fault**
THE CLEVEREST MAN - **The one who always does what he thinks is right**
THE GREATEST COMFORT - **The knowledge that you have done your work well**
THE MEANEST FEELING OF WHICH ANY HUMAN IS CAPABLE - **Feeling envious of another's success**
THE GREATEST THING- BAR NONE - IN THE WORLD
Love. Love for family, home, friends, neighbors and for the land in which we enjoy our freedom.

☆ ☆ ☆ ☆ ☆

You can tell more about a person by what he says about others than you can by what others say about him.

> "It's what you learn after you know it all that counts."
> John Wooden
> UCLA Basketball

☆ ☆ ☆ ☆ ☆

"You know, whether it's in business, politics, education, or athletics, there has to be respect and loyalty for the leader. Success or failure depends on it. There are three questions from the leader that must be answered affirmatively by individual group members if the group needs assurance that it can reach its desired goal. Can I trust you? Are you committed? Do you respect or care about me? If the individuals can answer "yes" to their leader to these three questions, even greatness is within their grasp."
Lou Holtz

☆ ☆ ☆ ☆ ☆

Decision is a sharp knife that cuts clean and straight; indecision is a dull one that hacks and tears and leaves ragged edges behind it.
Gordon Graham

☆ ☆ ☆ ☆ ☆

A boss cannot <u>make</u> you do anything, but he can surely make you regret you didn't.

It matters not where you are today, but in what direction you are moving and where you will finish.

☆ ☆ ☆ ☆ ☆

TIME

Few people actually waste time - they misuse it. Misusing time means not delegating work, not scheduling days, not making decisions, not establishing priorities.

Effective, successful people are people who get maximum benefit from a minimum investment of time. They are aware that time is their greatest asset and that it must be used with the utmost discretion.

☆ ☆ ☆ ☆ ☆

One of the qualities I would certainly look for in an executive is whether he knows how to delegate properly. The inability to do this is, in my opinion (and in that of others I have talked with on this subject), one of the chief reasons executives fail. Another is their inability to make decisions effectively. These two personality lacks have contributed more to executive failure than any amount of know-how lacks. **J.C. Penney**

☆ ☆ ☆ ☆ ☆

Life is being, not having.

MANY OF LIFE'S FAILURES ARE MEN WHO DID NOT REALIZE HOW CLOSE THEY WERE TO SUCCESS WHEN THEY GAVE UP.

☆ ☆ ☆ ☆ ☆

Economics is extremely useful as a form of employment for economists.

☆ ☆ ☆ ☆ ☆

It's a funny thing about life: if you refuse to accept anything but the very best you will very often get it.
W. Somerset Maugham

☆ ☆ ☆ ☆ ☆

If better is possible, good is not enough.

☆ ☆ ☆ ☆ ☆

IT'S HELL TO WORK FOR A NERVOUS BOSS, ESPECIALLY WHEN YOU ARE THE ONE WHO IS MAKING HIM NERVOUS.

☆ ☆ ☆ ☆ ☆

Swallowing angry words is much easier than having to eat them.

ARE YOU WORKING TOO HARD?

Who isn't working too hard? Run through our tongue-in-cheek checklist below. If more than five of the points apply to you, maybe you are working too hard!

1. You rush home from your 9-to-5 job just in time to catch the 11 o'clock news.

2. You wake up at 7 A.M. and get dressed for work before you realize it's Saturday.

3. You answer your home phone "Acme Widget Company".

4. You eat breakfast, lunch and dinner at the office.

5. You wake up from a nightmare in which the copy machine is chasing you.

6. You buy more new underwear because you haven't had a chance to do your laundry.

7. You look forward to the weekends so you can catch up on work when the office is quiet.

8. You type your food-shopping list.

9. You keep an in/out box on your dresser.

10. Your dog doesn't recognize you.

11. You're on a first-name basis with all the night watchmen.

12. More of your personal belongings are at work than at home—dishes, shoes, plants, photos.

13. You have no time to look for a new job.

A DAY OFF...

So you want the day off? Let's take a look at what you are asking for:

There are **365** days per year available for work. There are **52** weeks per year in which you already have **2** days off per week, leaving **261** days available for work. Since you spend **16** hours each day away from work, you have used up **170** days, leaving only **91** days available. You spend **30** minutes each day on coffee break. That accounts for **23** days each year, leaving only **68** days available. With a one-hour lunch period each day, you have used up another **48** days, leaving only **22** days available for work. You normally spend **2** days per year on sick leave. This leaves you only **20** days available for work. We offer **5** holidays per year, so your available working time is down to **15** days. We generously give you **14** days vacation per year which leaves you only **1** day available for work, and I'll be damned if you're going to take that day off!!!

☆ ☆ ☆ ☆ ☆

THAT'S NOT MY JOB...

This is a story about four people named **Everybody**, **Anybody**, **Somebody** and **Nobody**.

There was an important job to be done and **Everybody** was sure that **Somebody** would do it. **Anybody** could have done it, but **Nobody** did it. **Somebody** got angry about that because it was **Everybody's** job. **Everybody** thought **Anybody** could do it, but **Nobody** realized that **Everybody** wouldn't do it. It ended up that **Everybody** blamed **Somebody** when **Nobody** did what **Anybody** could have done.

THE SECRETARY'S PRAYER

Dear Lord, I need help. Help me to be a good subordinate and help me to have the memory of an elephant, or one at least three years long. Help me by some miracle to be able to do six things at once, answer four telephones at the same time while typing a letter that must go out today. And, when that letter doesn't get signed until tomorrow, give me the strength to keep from going over the brink of hysteria. Never let me lose patience, even when the boss has me searching the files for hours for data that is later discovered in his desk.

Help me to have the intelligence of a college professor; help me to understand and carry out all instructions without any explanation. Let me know always just where the boss is, what he's doing, and when he will be back, even though he did leave without telling me where he was going. And when the year ends, please let me have the foresight not to destroy records that will be asked for in a few days, even though I have been told to destroy them.

Help me to keep a level head and my feet on the ground, so that my secretarial performance will be a proper reflection of the pioneer women who made a place for me in the business world, and those who established me in a profession.

☆ ☆ ☆ ☆ ☆

No person can ever be happy until he has learned to enjoy what he has and not to worry over what he does not have.

ENTHUSIASM IN YOUR WORK IS HALF THE BATTLE WON.

☆ ☆ ☆ ☆

What Is Hustle?

Hustle is doing something that everyone is absolutely certain can't be done.

Hustle is getting the order because you got there first, or stayed with it after everyone else gave up.

Hustle is shoe leather and elbow grease and sweat and missing lunch.

Hustle is getting prospects to say "yes" after they've said "no" twenty times.

Hustle is doing more unto a customer than the other guy is doing unto him.

Hustle is believing in yourself and the business you're in.

Hustle is the sheer joy of winning.

Hustle is being the sorest loser in town.

Hustle is hating to take a vacation because you might miss a piece of the action.

Hustle is heaven if you're a hustler.

Hustle is hell if you're not.

☆ ☆ ☆ ☆ ☆

The dictionary is the only place *success* comes before *work*.

☆ ☆ ☆ ☆ ☆

Life is a lot like tennis: the one who can serve best seldom loses.

If you don't get everything you want, think of the things you don't get that you don't want.

☆ ☆ ☆ ☆ ☆

The In's and Out's of Your Job

It's **IN** to care about your job; it's **OUT** to bite the hand that feeds you.
It's **IN** to be loyal to the company that pays you; it's **OUT** to breed discontent.
It's **IN** to give a little more than expected; it's **OUT** to split when you haven't finished the task at hand. It's **IN** to be courteous - to anticipate the needs of fellow employees and plan accordingly; it's **OUT** to operate on your own, disregarding your obligation to others.
It's **IN** to appreciate all the benefits we enjoy; it's **OUT** to take all the benefits without making the best of what remains
 It's **IN** to praise fellow workers, while they're alive to hear it; it's **OUT** to wait until their wakes to say something nice.
It's **IN** to communicate with each other; it's **OUT** to withhold what is necessary to operate a business. It's **IN** to contribute, to get involved, to remain active; it's **OUT** to be passive, and pessimistic and aloof.
It's **IN** to work and win; it's **OUT** to exist and lose.
It's **IN** to make productive the days that will never come back; it's **OUT** to let the days drift by and wonder why you died of boredom.
It's **IN** to love your job; it's **OUT** to endure it.

By Mary Sweeney

**If you can imagine it, you can achieve it.
If you can dream it, you can become it.**

☆ ☆ ☆ ☆ ☆

The Garden of Life

First, plant five rows of **P's**:
- Presence
- Promptness
- Preparation
- Perseverance
- Purity

Next, plant three rows of **squash**:
- **Squash** gossip
- **Squash** indifference
- **Squash** unjust criticism

Then plant five rows of **lettuce**:
- **Let us** be faithful to duty
- **Let us** be unselfish and loyal
- **Let us** obey the rules and regulations
- **Let us** be true to our obligations
- **Let us** love one another

No garden is complete without **turnups**:
- **Turn up** for meetings
- **Turn up** with a smile
- **Turn up** with determination to make everything count for something good and worthwhile.

☆ ☆ ☆ ☆ ☆

**SUCCESS IS GETTING WHAT YOU WANT,
HAPPINESS IS WANTING WHAT YOU GET.**

The tragedy of life is not that we die, but what dies inside a man while he lives.
Albert Schweitzer

☆ ☆ ☆ ☆ ☆

Successful salesmen make up their minds what they want and then go after it with everything in them.

☆ ☆ ☆ ☆ ☆

You Have to Have the Goods
You've got to have the goods, my man, if you want to finish strong;
A bluff may work a little while, but not for very long; A line of talk all by itself will seldom see you through;
 You've got to have the goods, my man, and nothing else will do.
The fight is pretty stiff, my man. I'd call it rather tough;
And all along the routes are wrecks of those who tried to bluff;
They could not back their lines of talk to meet the final test.
You've got to have the goods, my man, and that's no idle jest.

☆ ☆ ☆ ☆ ☆

THE BIGGEST SIN IN LIFE IS WASTING TIME

☆ ☆ ☆ ☆ ☆

Jumping to conclusions seldom leads to happy landings.

"BELIEF IS THE THERMOSTAT WHICH REGULATES SUCCESS"

☆ ☆ ☆ ☆ ☆

TEN RULES FOR SUCCESS

1. Find your own particular talent.
2. Be big.
3. Be honest.
4. Live with enthusiasm.
5. Don't let your possessions possess you.
6. Don't worry about your problems.
7. Look up to people when you can - down to no one.
8. Don't cling to the past.
9. Assume your full share of responsibility in the world.
10. Strive to be happy.

☆ ☆ ☆ ☆ ☆

Freedom is like a coin...

It has the word privilege on one side and responsibility on the other. It does not have privilege on both sides. There are too many today who want everything involved in privilege but many refuse to accept anything that approaches the sense of responsibility.

Joseph R. Sizoo

☆ ☆ ☆ ☆ ☆

The closest some people ever come to reaching their ideal is when they write their resumes.

God Chooses Ordinary Men For Extraordinary Work

☆ ☆ ☆ ☆ ☆

Let us not pray to be sheltered from dangers but to be fearless when facing them.

☆ ☆ ☆ ☆ ☆

Dear Lord,
In this battle that goes on through life, I ask but a field that is fair. A chance to compete with all in the strife, and courage to strive and dare.

And if I should win, let it be by this code. With my faith and my honor held high.
And if I should lose, let me stand by the road. And cheer as the winner goes by.

☆ ☆ ☆ ☆ ☆

Do the very best you can, and leave the outcome to God.

☆ ☆ ☆ ☆ ☆

Confidence is when you care enough to send the very best, *and you go yourself.*

Robert Orden

ANGER IS OFTEN MORE HARMFUL THAN THE INJURY THAT CAUSED IT.

☆ ☆ ☆ ☆ ☆

SLOW ME DOWN, LORD

Slow me down Lord, ease the pounding of my heart by the quieting of my mind. Steady my hurried pace with a vision of the eternal reach of time.

Give me, amid the confusion of the day, the calmness of the everlasting hills. Break the tensions of my nerves and muscles with the soothing music of the singing streams that live in my memory, help me to know the magical, restoring power of sleep.

Teach me the art of taking minute vacations, of slowing down to look at a flower, to chat with a friend, to pat a dog, to read a few lines from a good book.

Slow me down Lord, and inspire me to send my roots deep into the soil of life's enduring values that I may grow toward the stars to my greater destiny.

☆ ☆ ☆ ☆ ☆

Definition of an executive:
A man in any organization who has the courage to dream, the ability to organize, and the strength to execute.

☆ ☆ ☆ ☆ ☆

In simplest terms, a leader is one who knows where he wants to go, gets up, and goes.

Common sense is really not all that common.

☆ ☆ ☆ ☆ ☆

There is a big difference between
wanting to **and** willing to.

☆ ☆ ☆ ☆ ☆

Take Time

Take Time to think-
it is the source of power.

Take Time to play-
it is the secret of youth.

Take Time to read
it is the foundation of wisdom.

Take Time to pray
it is the greatest power on earth.

Take Time to love and be loved
it is a God-given privilege.

Take Time to be friendly
it is the road to happiness.

Take Time to laugh
it is the music of the soul.

☆ ☆ ☆ ☆ ☆

Lord, help me to remember that
nothing is going to happen to me
today that You and I can't handle.

What you are is God's gift to you. What you make of yourself is your gift to God.

☆ ☆ ☆ ☆ ☆

Footprints

One night a salesman had a dream, he dreamed he was walking along the beach with the Lord. Across the sky flashed scenes from his life. For each scene he noticed two sets of footprints in the sand, one belonging to him, the other belonging to the Lord.

When the last scene of his life flashed before him, he looked back at the footprints in the sand. He noticed that many times along the path of life there was only one set of footprints. He also noticed that it happened at the very lowest and saddest times in his life. This really bothered him and he questioned the Lord about it.

"Lord, you said that once I decided to follow you, you would walk with me all the way, but I noticed that during the most troublesome times in my life there is only one set of footprints. I don't understand why in times when I needed you most, you would leave me."

The Lord replied, "My precious, precious child, I love you and I would never, never leave you during your times of trial and suffering. When you see only one set of footprints, it was then that I carried you."

☆ ☆ ☆ ☆ ☆

GOD'S HELP IS JUST A PRAYER AWAY

The Station

Tucked away in our subconscious is an idyllic vision. We see ourselves on a long trip that spans the continent. We are traveling by train. Out the windows, we drink in the passing scene of cars on nearby highways, of children waving at a crossing, of cattle grazing on a distant hillside, of smoke pouring from a power plant, of row upon row of corn and wheat, of flat lands and valleys, of mountains and rolling hillsides, of city skylines and village hills.

But uppermost in our minds is the final destination. On a certain day at a certain hour we will pull into the station. Bands will be playing and flags will be waving. Once we get there so many wonderful dreams will come true, and pieces of our lives will fit together like a completed jigsaw puzzle. How restlessly we paced the aisles, damning the minutes for loitering - waiting, waiting, waiting for the station.

Sooner or later we must realize there is no station, no one place to arrive at once and for all. The true joy of life is the trip. The station is only a dream. It constantly outdistances us.

So stop pacing the aisles and counting the miles. Instead, climb more mountains, eat more ice cream, go barefoot more often, swim more rivers, watch more sunsets, laugh more, cry less. Life must be lived as we go along. The station will come soon enough.

☆ ☆ ☆ ☆ ☆

Life can only be understood backwards, but it must be lived forward.

THE RACE DOES NOT ALWAYS GO TO THE SWIFT BUT MOST OFTEN TO HE WHO KEEPS ON RUNNING.

☆ ☆ ☆ ☆ ☆

SPEAKING...Some basic rules:
1) Know what you're going to say in advance
2) Look your listeners in the eye
3) Take your time. Talk clearly, concisely, and deliberately
4) Use an outline instead of memorizing a speech
5) Be constructive. Stress the merits of your viewpoint, not the flaws in someone elses's.
6) Use visual aids to engage your audience's eyes as well as ears, and capitalize by using gestures to emphasize important points
7) Go beyond self-interest. Showing the audience how you can help them achieve what they want is much more effective than putting yourself in the limelight
8) Be specific
9) Be yourself. You can learn from others, but don't make the mistake of trying to imitate a successful orator
10) Use a positive approach
11) Stop at the right time. When you sense that you have scored your points and that the audience gets the message, stop talking.

Healthways

☆ ☆ ☆ ☆ ☆

"**God** will look us over not for medals, or diplomas, or degrees, but for *Scars*."

Edward Sheldon

IT TAKES ONLY TWO PERCENT

Have you been working like a horse? I've been thinking about that expression and at least one horse I can name has earned a pretty fair hourly rate. Someone has figured out that the race horse *Nashua* earned more than a million dollars in a total racing time that added up to less than one hour!

But there is something else here of interest. What is there about a horse like Nashua that made him such a consistent winner and made him so valuable? You'd probably pay a hundred times as much for a horse like Nashua as you would for an ordinary race horse. But is he a hundred times faster? No. To be a consistent winner and to be worth a hundred times as much as the average, he needed only to be consistent in finishing just ahead of the rest.

A writer in a national magazine made the assertion that the difference between the man of achievement and the man of mediocrity is a difference of only about *two percent* in study, application, interest, attention, and effort. Only about two percent separates the winner from the loser! A boxer can win the world's championship simply by winning one more round than his opponent — or even by being only a point or two ahead. And this narrow margin can make the difference between fame and fortune or never being heard of again! It's often a matter of only two percent. We have no idea of what a change we could make in our results if we would simply add that two percent more time and effort than the average person is willing to put in.

He who spends some time on his knees
has no trouble standing on his feet.

☆ ☆ ☆ ☆ ☆

Talent will get you to the top, but it takes character to keep you there.
John Wooden

☆ ☆ ☆ ☆ ☆

God gave us two ends to use:
**One to think with,
the other to sit with.**
Success depends on which one you choose:
**heads you'll win,
tails you'll lose.**

☆ ☆ ☆ ☆ ☆

A MAN ATTAINS IN THE MEASURE THAT HE ASPIRES (OR PERSPIRES)!
JAMES ALLEN

☆ ☆ ☆ ☆ ☆

The wayside of business is full of brilliant men who started out with a spurt and lacked the stamina to finish. Their places were taken by patient and unshowy plodders who never knew when to quit.
J.R. Todd

Lord,
when we are wrong, make us willing to change.
And when we are right, make us easy to live with.

☆ ☆ ☆ ☆ ☆

A salesman for a key-making machine entered a hardware store and gave the shopkeeper a demonstration.

"Isn't it a wonderful machine?" he asked.
"Yes, it is."
"It would be a marvelous investment and a great time-saver, wouldn't it?"
"Yes."
"Don't you think every hardware store ought to have one?"
"Yes."
"Well, why don't you buy it?"
"Well," said the shopkeeper, "why don't you ask me to?"

☆ ☆ ☆ ☆ ☆

I asked of life: *"What have you to offer me?"*
And the answer came: *"What have you to give?"*

☆ ☆ ☆ ☆ ☆

IT IS IMPOSSIBLE TO GET A TOEHOLD ON SUCCESS BY ACTING LIKE A HEEL.

☆ ☆ ☆ ☆ ☆

The difficulties of life are intended to make us better - not bitter.

SO MUCH OF WHAT WE CALL MANAGEMENT CONSISTS OF MAKING IT DIFFICULT FOR PEOPLE TO WORK.
 Peter Drucker

☆ ☆ ☆ ☆ ☆

MISERY

How to be miserable: **1.** Use "I" as often as possible. **2.** Always be sensitive to slights. **3.** Be jealous and envious. **4.** Think only about yourself. **5.** Talk only about yourself. **6.** Trust no one. **7.** Never forget a criticism. **8.** Always expect to be appreciated. **9.** Be suspicious. **10.** Listen greedily to what others say of you. **11.** Always look for faults in others. **12.** Do as little as possible for others. **13.** Shirk your duties if you can. **14.** Never forget a service you may have rendered. **15.** Sulk if people aren't grateful for your favors. **16.** Insist on consideration and respect. **17.** Demand agreement with your own views on everything. **18.** Always look for a good time. **19.** Love yourself first. **20.** Be selfish at all times.
 This formula is guaranteed to work.

☆ ☆ ☆ ☆ ☆

WE WERE NOT PUT ON THIS EARTH BY GOD TO MAKE JUST A LIVING BUT TO MAKE A LIFE.

☆ ☆ ☆ ☆ ☆

A good leader takes a little more than his share of the blame, a little less than his share of the credit.

WINNERS AND LOSERS: HOW THEY DIFFER
By Sydney Harris

1. A winner says: "Let's find out". A loser says: "No body knows".
2. When a winner makes a mistake he says: "It was my fault". When a loser makes a mistake he says: "It isn't my fault".
3. A winner isn't nearly as afraid of losing as a loser is secretly afraid of winning.
4. A winner goes through a problem; a loser goes around it and never gets past it.
5. A winner makes a commitment; a loser makes promises.
6. A winner listens; a loser just waits until it's his turn to talk.
7. A winner feels strong enough to be gentle; a loser is never gentle, he is either weak or petty.
8. A winner respects those who are superior to him and tries to learn something from them; a loser resents those who are superior to him and tries to find chinks in their armor.
9. A winner explains; a loser complains.
10. A winner feels responsible for more than his job; a loser says, "I only work here."
11. A winner says: "There ought to be a better way to do it". A loser says: "That's the way it's always been done".
12. A winner paces himself; a loser has only two speeds: hysterical and lethargic.
13. A winner says: "I'm good, but not as good as I ought to be". A loser says: "I'm not as bad as a lot of other people".

When looking back, most of us are more sorry for the things we didn't do than for the things we shouldn't have done.

☆ ☆ ☆ ☆ ☆

What Are You Doing Now?

It matters not if you lost the fight and were badly beaten, too.
It matters not if you failed outright in the things you tried to do.
It matters not if you toppled down from the azure heights of blue,
But what are you doing now????

It matters not if your plans were foiled and your hopes have fallen through.
It matters not if your chance was spoiled for the gain almost in view.
It matters not if you missed the goal though you struggled brave and true...
But what are you doing now????

It matters not if your fortune's gone and your fame has vanished, too.
It matters not if a cruel world's score be directed straight at you.
It matters not if the worst has come and your dreams have not come true...
But what are you doing now????

R. Rhodes Stabley

☆ ☆ ☆ ☆ ☆

I shall pass through this world but once. Any good that I can do, or any kindness that I can show any human being, let me do it now and not defer it, for I shall not pass this way again.

It is one thing to itch for something and another to scratch for it.

☆ ☆ ☆ ☆ ☆

Guidelines for Success at any Age:

There are no rules that guarantee success at any age. However, psychologist and author Marilyn Machlowitz has studied 60 early achievers and has these tips:

• Seek, see and seize opportunities. Great chances and challenges don't always come gift-wrapped.

• Channel your passion into your profession. Don't expect success to satisfy all your dreams. Success doesn't make everything better.

• Persist and persevere. Overnight success is a myth.

• Be inquisitive. Read widely outside of your field. Ask questions and turn things inside out.

• Be optimistic. Things aren't always as hard to accomplish as you expect.

• Forget about a mentor. Multiple sponsors are a better bet.

• Don't worry about the downside of success. The problem of early success is exaggerated. Success removes the pressure to prove yourself.

• Derive some of your self-esteem from sources outside of work, so when things go badly, your balance won't be completely thrown off.

☆ ☆ ☆ ☆ ☆

DO UNTO OTHERS AS if OTHERS WERE YOU.

Happy is the person who can laugh at himself. He will never cease to be amused.
>   Habib Bourguiba

☆ ☆ ☆ ☆ ☆

WHY WORRY?

There are only two things to worry about; either you are well or you are sick. If you are well, then there is nothing to worry about. But if you are sick, there are two things to worry about; either you will get well, or you will die. If you get well, there is nothing to worry about. If you die, there are only two things to worry about; either you will go to Heaven or Hell. If you go to Heaven, there is nothing to worry about. But if you go to Hell, you'll be so busy shaking hands with friends you won't have time to worry.

☆ ☆ ☆ ☆ ☆

WE ALL MAKE MISTAKES -- ESPECIALLY THOSE WHO *DO* THINGS.

☆ ☆ ☆ ☆ ☆

There's no thrill in easy sailing, when the skies are clear and blue. There's no joy in merely doing things which anyone can do. But there is some satisfaction that is mighty sweet to take, when you reach a destination that you thought you couldn't make!

The wind blows the strongest upon those who stand the tallest.
F.C. Hayes

☆ ☆ ☆ ☆ ☆

LET SOMETHING GOOD BE SAID
James W. Riley

When over the fair fame of friend or foe, the shadow of disgrace shall fall; instead of words of blame, or proof of so and so, let something good be said.

Forget not that no fellow being yet may fall so low but love may lift his head; even the check of shame with tears is wet, if something good be said.

No generous heart may vainly turn aside in ways of sympathy; no soul so dead but may awaken strong and glorified, if something good be said.

And so I charge ye, by the thorny crown, and by the cross on which the Savior bled, and by your own soul's hope for fair renown, let something good be said.

☆ ☆ ☆ ☆ ☆

TIME WOUNDS ALL HEELS.

☆ ☆ ☆ ☆ ☆

Corporate growth is something
like riding on a bicycle.
If you coast very long, you fall off.

*A man who makes a mistake
and does not correct it
is committing another.*
　　　　　Confucius

☆ ☆ ☆ ☆ ☆

PRESS ON...

Nothing in the world can take the place of persistence.
Talent will not; nothing is more common than unsuccessful men with talent.
Genius will not; unrewarded genius is almost a proverb.
Education will not; the world is full of educated derelicts.
Persistence and determination alone are omnipotent.

☆ ☆ ☆ ☆ ☆

Four things never come back:
the **spoken word**, the **sped arrow**, the **past life** and the **neglected opportunity**.

☆ ☆ ☆ ☆ ☆

As a general rule, the most successful man in life is the man who has the best information.
　　　　　Disraeli

A man's reputation is the opinion people have of him, his character is what he really is.

Jack Miner

✩ ✩ ✩ ✩ ✩

SHOW ME

I'd rather see a lesson than to hear one any day,
I'd rather you'd walk with me than to merely
show me the way.
The eye's a better teacher and more willing
than the ear, and counsel is confusing but
examples always clear.
The best of all the teachers are the ones who live
the deeds, to see the good in action is what
everybody needs.
I soon can learn to do it if you let me see it
done, I can see your hand in action but
your tongue too fast may run.
And the counsel you are giving may be very
fine and true, but I'd rather get my lesson
by observing what you do!

✩ ✩ ✩ ✩ ✩

Treat people nicely on the way up, you're liable to meet them again on the way down.

Any fool can criticize, condemn, complain and most fools do!
Dale Carnegie

☆ ☆ ☆ ☆ ☆

It's All In A State of Mind

If you think you are beaten, you are; if you think you dare not, you won't; if you like to win, but don't think you can, it's almost a cinch you won't.

If you think you'll lose, you're lost; for out in the world you'll find success begins with a fellow's will.

It's all in a state of mind.

For many a game is lost ere even a play is run, and many a coward fails ere even his work is begun. Think big and your deeds will grow, think small and you'll fall behind; think that you can and you will;

It's all in a state of mind.

If you think you are out-classed you are; you've got to think high to rise; you've got to be sure of yourself before you can ever win a prize.

Life's battles don't always go to the stronger or faster man, but sooner or later, the man who wins is the fellow who thinks he can.

Walter D. Winkle

☆ ☆ ☆ ☆ ☆

We make our decisions, and then our decisions turn around and make us.

F.W. Boreham

"LUCK IS ALWAYS AGAINST THE MAN WHO DEPENDS ON IT."

☆ ☆ ☆ ☆ ☆

DON'T QUIT

When things go wrong, as they sometimes will, when the road you're trudging seems all uphill, when the funds are low and the debts are high and you want to smile but you have to sigh, when care is pressing you down a bit - rest if you must, but don't you quit.

Life is queer with its twists and turns as everyone of us sometimes learns. And many a fellow turns about when he might have won had he stuck it out. Don't give up though the pace seems slow - you may succeed with another blow.

Often the goal is nearer than it seems to a faint and faltering man; often the struggler has given up when he might have captured the victor's cup and he learned too late when the night came down how close he was to the golden crown.

Success is failure turned inside out, the silver tint of the clouds of doubt, and when you never can tell how close you are, it may be near when it seems afar; so stick to the fight when you're hardest hit - it's when things seem worst, you mustn't quit.

☆ ☆ ☆ ☆ ☆

Every person you meet is better at something than you are.

**One cannot always be a hero,
one can always be a man.**

☆ ☆ ☆ ☆ ☆

THE STUFF

The test of a man is the fight he makes, the grit that he daily shows, the way he stands on his feet and takes fate's numerous bumps and blows. A coward can smile when there's naught to fear, when nothing his progress bars; but it takes a man to stand and cheer while some other fellow soars.

It isn't the victory after all, but the fight that a brother makes; the man, who, driven against a wall, still stands up erect and takes the blows of fate with his head up high, bleeding and bruised and pale, is the man who will win in the by and by, for he ain't afraid to fail.

It's the bumps you get and the jolts you get, and the shocks that your courage stands, the hours of sorrow and vain regret, the prize that escaped your hands, that test your mettle and prove your worth; it isn't the blows you deal, but the blows you take on the good old earth that show if your stuff is real.

☆ ☆ ☆ ☆ ☆

"The tougher the job the greater the reward."

☆ ☆ ☆ ☆ ☆

No one can cheat you out of ultimate success but yourself.   Emerson

REPUTATION IS WHAT MEN THINK YOU ARE.
CHARACTER IS WHAT GOD KNOWS YOU ARE.

☆ ☆ ☆ ☆ ☆

FROM THE CAMP OF THE BEATEN
By Grantland Rice

I have learned something well worthwhile that victory could not bring: to wipe the blood from my mouth and smile where none can see the sting. I can walk, head up, while my heart is down from the beating that brought its good, and that means more than the champion's crown who is taking the easier road.

I have learned something worth far more than victory brings to men: battered and beaten, bruised and sore, I can still come back again. Crowded back in the hard, tough race, I've found that I have the heart to look raw failure in the face and train for another start.

Winners who wear the victor's wreath, looking for softer ways, watch for my blade as it leaves the sheath; sharpened on rougher days, trained upon pain and punishment, I've groped my way through the night, but the flag still flies from my battle tent and I've only begun to fight...

☆ ☆ ☆ ☆ ☆

Character is much easier kept than recovered.

**A diamond cannot be polished
without friction,
nor a man perfected without trials.**

☆ ☆ ☆ ☆ ☆

JUST THINK!

Just think! Some night the stars will gleam upon a cold, grey stone, and trace a name with silver beam, and lo! 'twill be your own.

That night is speeding on to greet your epitaphic rhyme. Your life is but a little beat within the heart of Time.

A little gain, a little pain, a laugh, lest you may moan; a little blame, a little fame, a star-gleam on a stone.

By Robert Service

☆ ☆ ☆ ☆ ☆

WHEN A MAN IMAGINES THAT HE HAS ATTAINED PERFECTION HIS DECLINE BEGINS.

☆ ☆ ☆ ☆ ☆

As C.S. Lewis wrote:
"If individuals live only 70 years, then a state, or a nation, or a civilization, which may last for a thousand years, is more important than an individual.

But if Christianity is true, then the individual is more important, for He is everlasting and the life of a state or civilization, compared with His, is only a moment."

LEADERSHIP USUALLY BEGINS WITH A VISION
OF SUCCESS, A GLIMMERING INTUITION THAT
SOLUTIONS TO PROBLEMS ARE POSSIBLE.

☆ ☆ ☆ ☆ ☆

If you are made of the right stuff,
a hard fall results in a high bounce.

☆ ☆ ☆ ☆ ☆

SUCCESS

He has achieved success who has lived well, laughed often, and loved much; who has gained the respect of intelligent men, and the love of little children; who has filled his niche and accomplished his task; who has never lacked appreciation of earth's beauty, or failed to express it; who has always looked for the best in others and given the best he had; whose life was an inspiration; whose memory a benediction.

By Bessie A. Stanley

☆ ☆ ☆ ☆ ☆

Inside inefficiency is more to be
feared than outside competition.

☆ ☆ ☆ ☆ ☆

BUSINESS TENDS TO SELECT TOP MEN FOR THEIR
CHARACTER AND CAPACITY, THEN OVERLOAD
THEM ACCORDING TO THEIR WILLINGNESS.

THERE IS NO MISTAKE SO GREAT AS THE MISTAKE OF NOT GOING ON.

☆ ☆ ☆ ☆ ☆

THE INDISPENSABLE MAN

Sometime when you're feeling important, sometime when your ego's in bloom, sometime when you take it for granted you're the best qualified in the room, sometime when you feel your going would leave an unfillable hole, just follow this simple instruction and see how it humbles your soul:

Take a bucket and fill it with water, put your hand in up to your wrist. Take it out and the hole that's remaining is a measure of how you'll be missed. You can splash all you please as you enter, you can stir up the water galore, but stop and you'll see in a minute that it looks quite the same as before.

There's a moral in this quaint expression, just do the best that you can, be proud of yourself, but remember there is no indispensable man.

☆ ☆ ☆ ☆ ☆

The minute you get the idea you're indispensable, you aren't.

☆ ☆ ☆ ☆ ☆

MEN DO NOT **FAIL,** THEY JUST **GIVE UP EASY.**

Unless you try to do something beyond what you have already done and mastered, you will never grow...

☆ ☆ ☆ ☆ ☆

ANYTIME YOU FEEL LIKE QUITTING... throughout your career, perhaps you'll remember this story of one of our people:

He failed in business in '32. He ran as a state legislator and lost in '32. He tried business again and failed in '33. His sweetheart died in '35. He had a nervous breakdown in '36. He ran for state elector in '40 after he regained his health. He was defeated for congress in '43, defeated again for congress in '48, defeated when he ran for senate in '55 and defeated for vice president of the United States in '56. He ran for the senate again in '58 and lost. This man never quit. He kept trying until the last. In 1860, this man, **Abraham Lincoln**, was elected President of the United States of America.

☆ ☆ ☆ ☆ ☆

When success turns a person's head, he's facing failure.

If you never have failed, it's an even guess you never have won a high success.

☆ ☆ ☆ ☆

SO YOU HAD A BAD DAY...

You're sick of the game? Why, that's a shame; you're young, you're brave and you're bright. You have had a raw deal, I know, but don't squeal, buck up! Do your darndest and fight! It's the plugging away that will win you the day. So don't be a piker 'ole pard; just call on your grit, it's so easy to quit. It's keeping on living that's hard.

It's easy to cry that you're beaten and die. It's easy to crawfish and crawl, but to fight and to fight when hope's out of sight, why, that's the best game of them all. And although you come out of each grueling bout all broken and beaten and scarred, just give one more try; it's so easy to die, it's keeping your chin up that's hard.

Robert Service

☆ ☆ ☆ ☆

There is so much that is bad in the best of us, and so much that is good in the worst of us that it doesn't behoove any of us to talk about the rest of us.

☆ ☆ ☆ ☆

Thinking is like living and dying. Each of us has to do it for himself.

Too many fellows think they can push themselves forward by patting themselves on the back.

☆ ☆ ☆ ☆ ☆

Buck Nystrom's Four Corners of Success:

1. COMMITMENT   2. EFFORT

SUCCESS

3. MOTIVATION   4. DISCIPLINE

☆ ☆ ☆ ☆ ☆

**WOULD THE BOY YOU WERE
BE PROUD OF THE MAN YOU ARE?**

☆ ☆ ☆ ☆ ☆

In England, the president of a vacuum cleaner company was explaining his talent for hiring top salesmen. "I give the new applicant a special test. I send him out to rent a flat while carrying a tuba."

☆ ☆ ☆ ☆ ☆

You can tell a company by the men it keeps.
W.A. Clarke

> Coming together is a beginning
> Keeping together is progress
> Working together is success.
> Henry Ford

☆ ☆ ☆ ☆ ☆

What is Class?

Class never runs scared. It is sure footed and confident in the knowledge that you can meet life head on and handle whatever comes along. Class never makes excuses. It takes its lumps and learns from past mistakes. Class is considerate of others. It knows that good manners is nothing more than a series of petty sacrifices. Class bespeaks an aristocracy that has nothing to do with ancestors or money. The most affluent blueblood can be totally without class while the descendant of a Welsh miner may ooze class from every pore. Class never tries to build itself up by tearing others down. Class is already up and need not strive to look better by making others look worse. Class can walk with kings and keep its virtue and talk with crowds and keep the common touch. Everyone is comfortable with the person who has class because he is comfortable with himself. If you have class you don't need much of anything else. If you don't have class, no matter what else you have doesn't make much difference.

☆ ☆ ☆ ☆ ☆

NO RULE FOR SUCCESS WILL WORK IF YOU DON'T.

So live that you wouldn't be ashamed to sell the family parrot to the town gossip.
　　　　　Will Rogers

☆ ☆ ☆ ☆ ☆

Nine Ways To Change People Without Giving Offense or Arousing Resentment:

1. Begin with praise and honest appreciation.
2. Call attention to people's mistakes indirectly.
3. Talk about your own mistakes before criticizing the other person.
4. Ask questions instead of giving orders.
5. Let the other man save his face.
6. Praise the slightest improvement and praise every improvement. Be hearty in your approbation and lavish in your praise.
7. Give the other person a fine reputation to live up to.
8. Use encouragement. Make the fault seem easy to correct.
9. Make the other person happy about doing the thing you suggest.

☆ ☆ ☆ ☆ ☆

If you don't take the time to find out what you're all about, you'll never know what life is all about.

"Don't Count The Days, Make The Days Count."

☆ ☆ ☆ ☆ ☆

If I Had A Boy...

If I had a boy, I would say this to him: "Son, be fair and be square in the race you most run, be brave if you lose and meek if you win; be better and nobler than I've been; be honest and fearless in all that you do, and honor the name I have given you."

If I had a boy I would want him to know, we reap in this life just about as we sow; and we get what we earn, be it little or great - regardless of luck and regardless of fate. I would teach him and show him the best that I could, that it pays to be honest and upright and good.

- Frank Carleton Nelson

☆ ☆ ☆ ☆ ☆

Inability to tell good from evil is the greatest worry of a man's life.

☆ ☆ ☆ ☆ ☆

IF GOOD MEN WERE ONLY BETTER, WOULD WICKED MEN BE SO BAD?
- J.W. Chadwick

The reason some men do not succeed is because their wishbone is where their backbone ought to be.

☆ ☆ ☆ ☆ ☆

Remember This:

If you work for a man, in Heaven's name, *work* for him. If he pays you wages which supply you bread and butter, work for him, speak well of him, stand by him and the institutions he represents.

If you must vilify, condemn and eternally disparage, resign your position and when you are outside, damn to your heart's content.

But as long as you are part of the institution do not condemn it.

If you do, you are loosening the tendrils that are holding you to the institution, and at the first high wind, you will be unprotected and blown away, and will probably never know why.

Elbert Hubbard

☆ ☆ ☆ ☆ ☆

HE WHO LOSES MONEY LOSES MUCH;
HE WHO LOSES FRIENDS LOSES MORE;
HE WHO LOSES FAITH LOSES ALL.

☆ ☆ ☆ ☆ ☆

NOTHING IS OPENED BY MISTAKE
AS OFTEN AS ONE'S MOUTH.

"TRUE GREATNESS CONSISTS OF BEING GREAT IN LITTLE THINGS."

☆ ☆ ☆ ☆ ☆

IF YOU THINK YOU'RE CONFUSED, CONSIDER POOR COLUMBUS. HE DIDN'T KNOW WHERE HE WAS GOING, WHEN HE GOT THERE, HE DIDN'T KNOW WHERE HE WAS AND WHEN HE GOT BACK HE DIDN'T KNOW WHERE HE HAD BEEN.

☆ ☆ ☆ ☆ ☆

Success consists of doing the common things uncommonly well.

☆ ☆ ☆ ☆ ☆

To him who tries and fails and quits, I am the foul blow. But to him who, in defeat the lessons of life would learn, I lead through darkness and disaster to where the scarlet lights of triumph burn.

☆ ☆ ☆ ☆ ☆

Have ideals and live with them.

☆ ☆ ☆ ☆ ☆

Many who are climbing the ladder of success have their ladder leaning against the wrong wall.

DON'T LOOK FOR MIRACLES.
YOU *ARE* A MIRACLE.

☆ ☆ ☆ ☆ ☆

THE LOST MASTER

"And when I come to die," he said,
"Ye shall not lay me out in state,
Nor leave your laurels at my head,
Nor cause your men of speech orate;
No monument your gift shall be,
No column in the Hall of Fame;
But just this line ye grave for me:
'He played the game.'"

So when his glorious task was done,
It was not of his fame we thought;
It was not of his battles won,
But of the pride with which he fought;
But of his zest, his ringing laugh,
His trenchant scorn of praise or blame:
And so we graved his epitaph,
"He played the game."

And so we, too, in humbler ways
Went forth to fight the fight anew,
And heeding neither blame nor praise,
We held the course he set us true.
And we, too, find the fighting sweet;
And we, too, fight for fighting's sake;
And though we go down in defeat,
And though our stormy hearts may break,
We will not do our Master shame:
We'll play the game, please God,
We'll play the game.
By Robert Service

IN BUSINESS, CONCEIT IS A QUEER DISEASE.
IT MAKES EVERYONE SICK EXCEPT THE
ONE WHO HAS IT.

☆ ☆ ☆ ☆ ☆

"Self respect cannot be hunted. It cannot be purchased. It is never for sale. It cannot be fabricated out of public relations. It comes to us when we are alone, in quiet moments, in quiet places, when we suddenly realize that, knowing the good, we have done it; knowing the beautiful, we have served it; knowing the truth, we have spoken it."
A. Whitney Griswald

☆ ☆ ☆ ☆ ☆

The best eraser in the world is a good night's sleep.

☆ ☆ ☆ ☆ ☆

Give me a man who holds on when others let go, who pushes ahead when others turn back, who stiffens up when others retreat, who knows no such words as 'can't' or 'quit' and I'll show you a man who will win in the end.

☆ ☆ ☆ ☆ ☆

A professional is one who does his best work when he feels the least like working.
F.L. Wright

MATURITY

Maturity is the ability to tolerate an injustice without wanting to get even. Maturity is patience. It is the willingness to postpone immediate gratification in favor of long-term gain. Maturity is perseverance, sweating out a project in the face of heavy opposition and discouraging setbacks. Maturity is the capacity to face unpleasantness and frustration, discomfort and defeat without complaint, collapse or attempting to find someone to blame. Maturity is humility. It is being big enough to say, "I was wrong." And when right, the mature person is able to forego the satisfaction of saying, "I told you so."

Maturity is the ability to evaluate a situation, make a decision and stick with it. The immature spend their lives exploring possibilities, changing their minds and in the end they do nothing. Maturity means dependability, keeping one's word, coming through in a crisis. The immature are masters of the alibi. They are confused and disorganized. Their lives are a maze of broken promises, former friends, unfinished business and good intentions that never materialized.

Maturity is the art of living in peace with that which we cannot change, the courage to change that which can be changed and the wisdom to know the difference.

Triumph is just **umph** added to **try!**

☆ ☆ ☆ ☆

The man who is bigger than his job, keeps his cool, does not lose his head, refuses to become rattled, to fly off in a temper. The man who would control others must be able to control himself. There is something admirable, something inspiring, something soul-stirring about a man who displays coolness and courage under extremely trying circumstances. A good temper is not only a business asset, it is the secret of health. The longer you live, the more you will learn that a disordered temper breeds a disordered body.

B.C. Forbes

☆ ☆ ☆ ☆

SUCCESS... DEMANDS SINGLENESS OF PURPOSE

☆ ☆ ☆ ☆

If things are not going well with you, begin correcting the situation by carefully examining the service you are rendering, and especially the spirit in which you are rendering it.

Roger Babson

The people most preoccupied with titles and status are usually the least deserving of them.

☆ ☆ ☆ ☆ ☆

WE NEED MEN...

Who cannot be bought...
...whose word is their bond...who put character above wealth...who possess opinions and a will ...who are larger than their vocations. ...who do not hesitate to take chances.
...who will make no compromise with wrong. ...who will not lose their individuality in a crowd. ...who will be as honest in small things as in great things.
...who will not say they do it "because everybody else does it." ...whose ambitions are not confined to their own selfish desires. ...who give thirty-six inches to the yard and thirty-two quarts to the bushel. ...who will not have one brand of honesty for business purposes and another for private life.
...who are true to their friends through good report and evil report, in adversity as well as in prosperity.
...who do not believe that shrewdness, sharpness, cunning and strong headedness are the best qualities for winning success.
...who are not ashamed or afraid to stand for the truth when it is unpopular...who can say **"no"** with emphasis even though all the rest of the world says **"yes"**.

DISCIPLINE IS THE REFINING FIRE BY WHICH TALENT BECOMES ABILITY.

☆ ☆ ☆ ☆ ☆

The six mistakes of man:

1) The delusion that personal gain is made by crushing others.
2) The tendency to worry about things that can not be changed or corrected.
3) Insisting that a thing is impossible because we cannot accomplish it.
4) Refusing to set aside trivial preferences.
5) Neglecting development and refinement of the mind, and not acquiring the habit of reading and study.
6) Attempting to compel others to believe and live as we do.

Cicero

☆ ☆ ☆ ☆ ☆

DO IT LIKE IT IS YOUR LAST CHANCE

☆ ☆ ☆ ☆ ☆

Some people are so busy learning the *tricks* of the trade that they never learn the *trade*.

☆ ☆ ☆ ☆ ☆

We do not remember days,
we remember moments.

CAN'T

CAN'T is the worst word that's written or spoken; doing more harm here than slander and lies; on it is many a strong spirit broken, and with it many a good purpose dies. It springs from the lips of the thoughtless each morning and robs us of courage we need through the day. It rings in our ears like a timely-sent warning and laughs when we falter and fall by the way.

CAN'T is the father of feeble endeavor, the parent of terror and half-hearted work; it weakens the efforts of artisans clever, and makes of the toiler an indolent shirk. It poisons the soul of the man with a vision; it stifles in infancy many a plan; it greets honest toiling with open derision and mocks at the hopes and the dreams of a man.

CAN'T is a word none should speak without blushing; to utter it should be a symbol of shame; ambition and courage it daily is crushing; it blights a man's purpose and shortens his aim, despise it with all of your hatred of error; refuse it the lodgement it seeks in your brain; arm against it as a creature of terror, and all that you dream of you some day shall gain.

CAN'T is the word that is foe to ambition, an enemy ambushed to shatter your will; its prey is forever the man with a mission and bows but to courage and patience and skill. Hate it, with hatred that's deep and undying, for once it is welcomed 'twill break any man; whatever the goal you are seeking, keep trying and answer this demon by saying, **"I CAN."**

Edgar A. Guest

I have never heard of anyone stumbling onto something big while sitting down.

☆ ☆ ☆ ☆ ☆

YOU CANNOT DO A KINDNESS TOO SOON
FOR YOU NEVER KNOW HOW SOON
IT WILL BE TOO LATE.

☆ ☆ ☆ ☆ ☆

The time to make friends is before you need them.

☆ ☆ ☆ ☆ ☆

It is becoming more and more apparent that we **rust out** instead of **wear out.** Physical and mental activity are vital if we wish to prolong the youthful portion of life and enjoy later years.

☆ ☆ ☆ ☆ ☆

A FAULT RECOGNIZED IS HALF CORRECTED.

☆ ☆ ☆ ☆ ☆

Our grand business is not to see what lies dimly at a distance, but to do what lies clearly at hand.
Thomas Carlyle

Good Leaders Were First Great Followers.

☆ ☆ ☆ ☆ ☆

A LITTLE MORE...

The line between failure and success is so fine that we scarcely know when we pass it — so fine that we are often on the line and we do not know it.

How many a man has thrown up his hands at a time when a little more effort, a little more patience, would have achieved success!

As the tide goes clear out, so it comes clear in. In business, sometimes prospects may seem darkest when really they are on the turn. A *little* more persistence, a *little* more effort, and what seemed a hopeless failure may turn to glorious success.

There is no defeat except in no longer trying. There is no defeat save from within, no really insurmountable barrier, save our own inherent weakness of purpose.

Elbert Hubbard

☆ ☆ ☆ ☆ ☆

It's amazing how much can be accomplished if no one cares who gets the credit.

☆ ☆ ☆ ☆ ☆

GOOD ACTIONS GET GOOD RESULTS IN TIME.

OPPORTUNITY
By Walter Malone

They do me wrong who say I come no more when once I knock and fail to find you in. For every day I stand outside your door and bid you wake, and rise to fight and win. Wail not for precious chances passed away, wail not for golden ages on the wane! Each night I burn the records of that day; and at sunrise every soul is born again.

☆ ☆ ☆ ☆ ☆

Before strongly desiring anything, we should look carefully into the happiness of its owner.
- La Rochefoucauld

☆ ☆ ☆ ☆ ☆

Do all the good you can by all the means you can in all the ways you can in all the places you can at all the times you can to all the people you can as long as you can.

☆ ☆ ☆ ☆ ☆

Realize...
nothing is learned while you talk.

> **Neither you nor the world knows what you can do until you have tried.**
>
> Ralph Waldo Emerson

☆ ☆ ☆ ☆ ☆

KEEP ON KEEPIN' ON...

If the day looks kinder gloomy and your chances kinder slim, and the situation's puzzlin', and the prospect awful grim, and perplexities keep a-pressin' till all hope is nearly gone just bristle up and grit your teeth and keep on keepin' on.

Fumin' never wins a fight, and frettin' never pays; There ain't no good in broodin' in those pessimistic ways; smile just kinder cheerfully when hope is nearly gone, and bristle up and grit your teeth and keep on keepin' on.

There ain't no use in growlin' and grumblin' all the time, when the music's ringin' everywhere, and everything's in rhyme; Just keep on smilin' cheerfully if hope is nearly gone, and bristle up and grit your teeth and keep on keepin' on.

Even a mosquito doesn't get a slap on the back until he starts to work.

☆ ☆ ☆ ☆ ☆

Ten Commandments of Business:

1. Handle the hardest job first each day. Easy ones are pleasures.
2. Do not be afraid of criticism - criticize yourself often.
3. Be glad and rejoice in the other fellow's success - study his methods.
4. Do not be misled by dislikes. Acid ruins the finest fabrics.
5. Be enthusiastic - it is contagious.
6. Do not have the notion that success means simply money-making.
7. Be fair, and do at least one decent act every day.
8. Humor the chief. There must be a head to everything.
9. Have confidence in yourself; believe you can do it.
10. Harmonize your work. Let sunshine radiate and penetrate your relationships.

☆ ☆ ☆ ☆ ☆

WE CAN OFTEN DO MORE FOR OTHER MEN BY CORRECTING **OUR** OWN FAULTS THAN BY TRYING TO CORRECT **THEIRS.**

☆ ☆ ☆ ☆ ☆

The greatest risk in life is to wait for and depend upon others for your security.

> The most valuable gift you can give another is a good example.

☆ ☆ ☆ ☆

THE OPTIMIST VS. THE PESSIMIST

The optimist turns the impossible into the possible; the pessimist turns the possible into the impossible.

The optimist pleasantly ponders how high his kite will fly; the pessimist woefully wonders how soon his kite will fall.

The optimist sees a green near every sand trap; the pessimist sees a sand trap near every green.

The optimist looks at the horizon and sees an opportunity; the pessimist peers into the distance and fears a problem.

To the optimist all doors have handles and hinges; to the pessimist all doors have locks and latches. The optimist promotes progress, prosperity and plenty; the pessimist preaches limitations, liabilities and losses.

The optimist accentuates assets, abundance, and advantages; the pessimist majors in mistakes, misfortunes and misery.

The optimist goes out and finds the bell; the pessimist gives up and wrings his hands.

W.A. Ward

If there's one thing we should let others find out for themselves, it's how great we are.

☆ ☆ ☆ ☆ ☆

Make One More Call

I will persist until I succeed.
I was not delivered into this world in defeat,
nor does failure course through my veins.
I am not a sheep waiting to be prodded
by my shepherd.
I am a winner and I refuse to talk,
to walk with the sheep.
The slaughterhouse of failure is not my destiny.
I will persist until I succeed.

☆ ☆ ☆ ☆ ☆

I SEE NO VIRTUE WHERE I SMELL NO SWEAT.
FRANCIS QUARIES

☆ ☆ ☆ ☆ ☆

Beware of those who stand aloof
And greet each venture with reproof;
The world would stop if things were run
By men who say, "It can't be done!"

☆ ☆ ☆ ☆ ☆

We are all God-created, but self-molded.

YOU CAN GET ANYTHING IN THIS WORLD YOU WANT IF YOU HELP ENOUGH PEOPLE GET WHAT THEY WANT.

☆ ☆ ☆ ☆ ☆

The average person puts only 25 percent of his energy and ability into his work. The world takes off its hat to those who put in more than 50 percent of their capacity, and stands on its head for those few and far between souls who devote 100 percent.
Andrew Carnegie

☆ ☆ ☆ ☆ ☆

Set your goal higher than you can reach, then reach it.
Glenn Steward

☆ ☆ ☆ ☆ ☆

True friendship is like sound health: the value of it is seldom known until it is lost.
C.C. Colton

☆ ☆ ☆ ☆ ☆

"I don't know why people question the academic training of some business leaders. Half the doctors in the country graduated in the bottom half of their class."
Al McGuire

Make new friends in business but keep the old:
the first are silver, the latter gold.

☆ ☆ ☆ ☆ ☆

One man in a company plus courage, is a majority.

☆ ☆ ☆ ☆ ☆

The Clock Of Life

The clock of life is wound but once and no man has the power to tell when the hands will stop, at a late or early hour.
Now is the only time we own. Love, laugh, toil with a will. Do not wait until tomorrow, for the clock may then be still.

☆ ☆ ☆ ☆ ☆

DO YOU NOT KNOW THAT YOU ARE GOD'S TEMPLE AND THAT GOD'S SPIRIT DWELLS IN YOU?
1 Cor. 3:16

☆ ☆ ☆ ☆ ☆

We're All In This Together.

☆ ☆ ☆ ☆ ☆

It is not what you get that makes you successful, it is what you are continuing to do with what you've got.

WOMAN... Was made from the rib of man. She was not created from his head to top him, nor his feet to be stepped upon. She was made from his side to be equal to him; from beneath his arm, to be protected by him; near his heart, to be loved by him.

☆ ☆ ☆ ☆ ☆

God's Minute

I have only just a minute
only sixty seconds in it
forced upon me, can't refuse it
didn't seek it, didn't choose it
but it's up to me to use it.
It may suffer if I lose it
give account if I abuse it
just a tiny little minute
but eternity is in it.

☆ ☆ ☆ ☆ ☆

The reason so many people are unhappy today and seeking help to cope with life is that they fail to understand what human existence is all about. Until we recognize that life is not just something to be enjoyed, but rather is a task that each of us is assigned we'll never find meaning in our lives and never truly be happy.

Dr. Victor Frankl
Holocaust Survivor

YOU CAN'T TURN BACK THE CLOCK, BUT YOU CAN WIND IT UP AGAIN.

☆ ☆ ☆ ☆ ☆

IN BUSINESS...

Your success depends upon you. You have to steer your own course. **You** have to do your own thing. **You** must make your own decisions. **You** have to solve your own problems. **Your** character is your handiwork. **You** have to write your own record. **You** have to build your own monument or dig your own pit. **Which are you doing?**

B.C. Forbes

☆ ☆ ☆ ☆ ☆

57 Rules for Success:

First, deliver the goods.
Second, the other 56 don't matter.

☆ ☆ ☆ ☆ ☆

Even if you're on the right track, you'll get run over if you just sit there.

☆ ☆ ☆ ☆ ☆

TO ACHIEVE ALL THAT IS POSSIBLE, WE MUST ATTEMPT THE *IMPOSSIBLE.*

Three of the most difficult things in life are to:
- Keep a secret
- Forget an injury
- Make good use of leisure time

☆ ☆ ☆ ☆ ☆

THE RECKONING

It's fine to have a blow-out in a fancy restaurant, with terrapin and canvas-back and all the wine you want; to enjoy the flowers and music, watch the pretty women pass, smoke a choice cigar and sip the wealthy water in your glass. It's bully in a high-toned joint to eat and drink your fill, but it's quite another matter when you
Pay the bill.

It's great to go out every night on fun or pleasure bent; to wear your glad rags always and to never save a cent; to drift along regardless, have a good time every trip; to hit the high spots sometimes, and to let your chances slip; to know you're acting foolish, yet to go on fooling still, 'till Nature calls a show-down and you
Pay the bill.

Time has got a little bill - get wise while yet you may, for the debit side's increasing in a most alarming way; the things you had no right to do, the things you should have done, they're all put down; it's up to you to pay for every one. So eat, drink and be merry, have a good time if you will, but God help you when the time comes, and you
Foot the bill.
By Robert Service

A MAN WHO DARES TO WASTE ONE HOUR OF TIME HAS NOT DISCOVERED THE VALUE OF LIFE.
                        CHARLES DARWIN

☆ ☆ ☆ ☆ ☆

IN PURSUIT OF HAPPINESS...
Sooner or later, a man, if he is wise, discovers that life is a mixture of good days and bad, victory and defeat, give and take. He learns that it doesn't pay to be a sensitive soul; that he should let some things go over his head like water off a duck's back. He learns that he who loses his temper usually loses out.

He learns that carrying a chip on his shoulder is the easiest way to get into a fight. He learns that the quickest way to become unpopular is to carry tales and gossip about others. He learns that buck-passing always turns out to be a boomerang, and that it never pays. He comes to realize that the business could run along perfectly well without him. He learns that it doesn't matter so much who gets the credit so long as the business shows a profit. He learns that even the janitor is human and that it doesn't do any harm to smile and say "Good Morning" even if it is raining.
He learns that "getting along" depends about ninety-eight percent on his own behavior.

☆ ☆ ☆ ☆ ☆

Things don't matter as much as your attitude toward them.

IF
By Rudyard Ripling

If you can keep your head when all about you are losing theirs and blaming it on you; if you can trust yourself when all men doubt you, but make allowance for their doubting too; if you can wait and not be tired by waiting, or, being lied about, don't deal in lies, or being hated don't give way to hating, and yet don't look too good, nor talk too wise

If you can dream - and not make dreams your master; if you can think - and not make thoughts your aim, if you can meet with Triumph and Disaster and treat those two impostors just the same: if you can bear to hear the truth you've spoken twisted by knaves to make a trap for fools, or watch the things you gave your life to, broken, and stoop and build 'em up with worn-out tools;

If you can make one heap of all your winnings and risk it on one turn of pitch-and-toss, and lose, and start again at your beginnings and never breathe a word about your loss; if you can force your heart and nerve and sinew to serve your turn long after they are gone, and so hold on when there is nothing in you except the Will which says to them: "Hold on!"

If you can talk with crowds and keep your virtue, or walk with Kings - nor lose the common touch, if neither foes nor loving friends can hurt you, if all men count with you, but none too much: if you can fill the unforgiving minute with sixty seconds' worth of distance run, yours is the Earth and everything that's in it, and - which is more - **you'll be a Man, my son!**

THE QUITTER

When you're lost in the Wild, and you're scared as a child, and Death looks you bang in the eye, and you're sore as a boil, it's according to Hoyle to cock your revolver and...die. But the *Code of a Man* says: "Fight all you can," and self-dissolution is barred. In hunger and woe, oh, it's easy to blow...it's the *hell-served-for-breakfast* that's hard.

"You're sick of the game!" Well now, that's a shame. You're young and you're brave and you're bright. "You've had a raw deal!" I know - but don't squeal, buck up, do your damndest, and fight. It's the plugging away that will win you the day, so don't be a piker, old pard! Just draw on your grit; it's so easy to quit: it's the keeping-your-chin-up that's hard.

It's easy to cry that you're beaten and die; it's easy to crawfish and crawl; but to fight and to fight when hope's out of sight - why, that's the best game of them all! And though you come out of each grueling bout, all broken and beaten and scarred, just have one more try - it's dead easy to die, it's the keeping-on-living that's hard.

By Robert Service

☆ ☆ ☆ ☆ ☆

Never - Never - Never - NEVER GIVE UP!
W. Churchill

KEEP CLIMBING

Life is a struggle, a continual climb, if we're ever to reach our goal;
Requiring real effort from dawn to dusk, ere we slip and mar our soul.
For the road of life is rough and rugged, with many a stone in the way;
And only with courage and a will to win, can we reach the summit one day.
God never intended that the going be easy, that our pathway be strewn with flowers;
But by overcoming hardships day by day, we grow stronger in our various powers.   Then up with your chin and out with a smile, start pushing your way to the top;
The higher you climb, the better the view; keep right on going, never say stop.
There will be many on the road of life, to caution you of the dangers you face.
Suggesting you turn back, give up the goal, and with them your footsteps retrace.
Right then is the time to show your courage, and decide for once and for all;
That your life's task lies directly ahead, and on this decision, rise or fall.
Then in faith push on to heights sublime, not back to the land of ease;
You'll always find light, facing the sun, and shadows in the rear, if you please.
The higher you climb, the greater the zeal, more courage will be given if you ask;
Only be sure you're guided by truth, and He'll supply strength for the task.

WHAT IT TAKES TO BE NUMBER ONE
By Vince Lombardi

"Winning is not a sometime thing: it's an all-the-time thing. You don't win once in a while. You don't do things right once in a while. You do them right all the time. Winning is a habit. Unfortunately, so is losing.

Every time a football player goes out to ply his trade he's got to play from the ground up from the soles of his feet right up to his head. Every inch of him has to play. Some guys play with their heads - that's O.K., you've got to be smart to be #1 in any business - but more important, you've got to play with your heart, with every fiber of your body. If you're lucky enough to find a guy with a lot of head and a lot of heart, he's never going to come off the field second.

It's a reality of life that men are competitive and the most competitive games draw the most competitive men. That's why they're there - to compete. They know the rules and the objectives when they get in the game. The objective is to win; fairly, squarely, decently, by the rules, but to **win**.

And in truth, I've never known a man worth his salt who in the long run, deep down in his heart, didn't appreciate the grind, the discipline. There is something in good men that really yearns for - *needs* - discipline and the harsh reality of head-to-head combat."

Excellence is Never an Accident

It is achieved in an institution only as a result of an unrelenting and vigorous insistence on the highest standards of performance. It requires an unswerving expectancy of quality from the staff and volunteers.

Excellence is contagious. It infects and affects everyone in the organization. It charts the direction of a program. It establishes the criteria for planning. It provides zest and vitality to the organization. Once achieved, excellence has a talent for permeating every aspect of the life of the organization.

Excellence demands commitment and a tenacious dedication from the leadership of the organization. Once it is accepted and expected, it must be nourished and continually reviewed and renewed. It is a never-ending process of striving and searching. It requires a spirit of mission and boundless energy. It is always the result of a creatively conceived and precisely planned effort.

Excellence is an organization's life-line. It is the most compelling answer to apathy and inertia. It energizes a stimulating and pulsating force. Once it becomes the expected standard of performance, it develops a fiercely driving and motivating philosophy of operation. Excellence is a state of mind put into action. It galvanizes an organization. It *incentivizes. Stimulates. Inspires.*
When a climate of excellence exists, all things - staff work, volunteer leadership, finances, program - are success driven.

The ladder of success doesn't care who climbs it.
Frank Tyger

☆ ☆ ☆ ☆ ☆

JUST FOR TODAY...

Just for today I will live through the next 12 hours and not tackle my whole life problem at once. Just for today I will improve my mind. I will learn something useful. I will read something that requires effort, thought and concentration.

Just for today, I will not find fault with a friend, relative or colleague. I will not try to change or improve anyone but myself.

Just for today I will have a program. I might not follow it exactly, but I will have it. I will save myself from two enemies - hurry and indecision.

Just for today I will exercise my character in three ways. I will do a good turn and keep it a secret. If anyone finds out, it won't count.

Just for today I will do two things I don't want to do, just for the exercise.

Just for today I will be unafraid. Especially will I be unafraid to enjoy what is beautiful and believe that as I give to the world, the world will give to me.

Ann Landers
Nationally Syndicated Column
October 1972

☆ ☆ ☆ ☆ ☆

To avoid criticism, say nothing, do nothing, be nothing.

IT'S GREAT TO BE GREAT, BUT IT'S GREATER TO BE HUMAN.
Will Rodgers

☆ ☆ ☆ ☆ ☆

The Only Way To Win
It takes a little courage, and a little self-control and some grim determination, if you want to reach your goal. It takes some real striving, and a firm and stern-set chin, no matter what the battle, if you really want to win. There's no easy path to glory, there's no rosy road to fame; life, however, we may view it, is no simple parlor game. But its prizes call for fighting, for endurance and for grit, for a rugged disposition and a "don't-know-when-to-quit". You must take a blow or give one, you must risk and you must lose; and expect that in the struggle you will suffer from the bruise. But you must not wince or falter, if a fight you once begin; be a man and face the battle that's the only way to win.

☆ ☆ ☆ ☆ ☆

One of the rarest things that a man ever does is the very best he can...

☆ ☆ ☆ ☆ ☆

Big Shots are usually Little Shots who kept on shooting.

Never put your finger on someone's faults unless it's part of a helping hand.

☆ ☆ ☆ ☆ ☆

Paradoxical Commandments of Leadership
1. People are illogical, unreasonable, and self-centered. **Love them anyway.**
2. If you do good, people will accuse you of selfish ulterior motives. **Do good anyway.**
3. If you are successful, you win false friends and true enemies. **Succeed anyway.**
4. The good you do today will be forgotten tomorrow. **Do good anyway.**
5. Honesty and frankness make you vulnerable. **Be honest and frank anyway.**
6. The biggest men with the biggest ideas can be shot down by the smallest men with the smallest ideas. **Think big anyway.**
7. People favor underdogs but follow only top dogs. **Fight for a few underdogs anyway.**
8. What you spend years building may be destroyed overnight. **Build anyway.**
9. People really need help but may attack you if you help them. **Help them anyway.**
10. Give the world the best you have and you'll get kicked in the teeth. **Give the world the best you have anyway.**

☆ ☆ ☆ ☆ ☆

SUCCESS COMES IN CANS, NOT IN CAN'TS!

Cripple him, and you have a Sir Walter Scott. Lock him in a prison cell, and you have a John Bunyan. Bury him in the snows of Valley Forge, and you have a George Washington. Raise him in abject poverty, and you have an Abraham Lincoln. Subject him to bitter religious prejudice, and you have a Disraeli. Afflict him with asthma as a child, and you have a Theodore Roosevelt. Stab him with rheumatic pains until he can't sleep without an opiate, and you have a Steinmetz. Put him in a grease pit of a locomotive roundhouse, and you have a Walter P. Chrysler. Make him play second fiddle in an obscure South American orchestra, and you have a Toscanini. At birth, deny her the ability to see, hear, and speak, and you have a Helen Keller.
      Abigail Van Buren

☆ ☆ ☆ ☆ ☆

Quitcherbellyakinangotowork!

☆ ☆ ☆ ☆ ☆

"IF AT FIRST YOU DON'T SUCCEED, YOU'RE DOING ABOUT AVERAGE."

☆ ☆ ☆ ☆ ☆

Besides pride, loyalty, discipline, heart and mind, confidence is the key to all the locks.
    Joe Paterno, Penn State

DON'T BELITTLE...BE BIG

☆ ☆ ☆ ☆ ☆

As in nature, as in art, so in grace; it is rough treatment that gives souls, as well as stones, their luster. The more the diamond is cut the brighter it sparkles; and in what seems hard dealing, there God has no end in view but to perfect his people.
K.S. Guthrie

☆ ☆ ☆ ☆ ☆

Do not pray for an easy life. Pray to be a strong person.

☆ ☆ ☆ ☆ ☆

The path to success is never a 5-lane, no-traffic, super highway. Heartbreaks, setbacks, frustrations, failures, enemies... appear time and again to prevent you from reaching your goals.
N.C. Stone

☆ ☆ ☆ ☆ ☆

I CAN OF MINE OWNSELF DO NOTHING.
John 5:30

☆ ☆ ☆ ☆ ☆

Experience tells you what to do; confidence allows you to do it.

> A winning habit is like a cable: a thread is woven each day until the product becomes **UNBREAKABLE!!**

☆ ☆ ☆ ☆ ☆

More on Maturity...

Maturity is the ability to base a judgement on the big picture, the long haul. Maturity is the ability to stick with a project or situation until it is finished. Maturity is the ability to face unpleasantness, frustration, discomfort and defeat without complaint or collapse. Maturity is the ability to live up to your responsibilities and this means being dependable, keeping your word. The world is filled with people who can't be counted on. People who never seem to come through in the clutches. People who break promises. Maturity is the ability to make a decision and stand by it. Maturity is the ability to harness your abilities and energies.

☆ ☆ ☆ ☆ ☆

THERE IS NO EASY WAY.

☆ ☆ ☆ ☆ ☆

> The trouble with the future is that it usually arrives before we are ready for it.

TO BE BORN A GENTLEMAN IS AN ACCIDENT; TO DIE ONE, AN ACHIEVEMENT.

☆ ☆ ☆ ☆ ☆

True Grit is making a decision and standing by it, doing what must be done - for no moral man can have peace of mind if he leaves undone what he knows he should have done.
          John Wayne

☆ ☆ ☆ ☆ ☆

You never get a second chance to make a good first impression.

☆ ☆ ☆ ☆ ☆

THE REAL WAY TO ENJOY LIFE IS AS A PARTICIPANT. PERHAPS IT'S THE PEOPLE WHO THINK THEY'RE SPECTATORS THAT SPREAD THE IDEA THAT ALL PLEASURE MUST BE PAID FOR. DON'T PAY FOR ANY OF IT...LIFE IS FREE.

☆ ☆ ☆ ☆ ☆

All money ever does is make you bigger than whatever it was you were before. If you were a nice man before, it makes you a bigger nice man. If you were a jerk, it makes you a bigger jerk.
          Bill Russell

Any life truly lived is a risky business, and if one puts up too many fences against the risks one ends by shutting out life itself.
–Kenneth S. Davis in a biography of
Dwight Eisenhower

☆ ☆ ☆ ☆ ☆

Innumerable symptoms of (executive) failure can be traced to four basic causes:

1. Lack of drive. This used to be attributed to laziness. More likely it is due to preoccupation, a bone-deep concern with other matters, physical and pyschological, that leave such a man powerless to concentrate on his job, unable to be motivated by it.

2. Deficiency of imagination. A good executive has the capacity to explore the future in fiction before he undertakes it in fact. He expects the unexpected.

3. Lack of common sense, and lack of perception and judgment; both essential to any successful human relationship.

4. Inability to communicate. He is disorganized, unfamiliar with his audience and his material. Because he cannot express himself with clarity and precision, he cannot be understood or he is misunderstood.

Roy Pearson

☆ ☆ ☆ ☆ ☆

THE HIGHER YOU GO IN LIFE, THE MORE YOU BECOME DEPENDENT ON OTHERS.

WHAT REALLY COUNTS IS NOT THE NUMBER OF HOURS YOU PUT IN, BUT HOW MUCH YOU PUT IN THE HOURS.

☆ ☆ ☆ ☆ ☆

WHEN IS A MAN EDUCATED?

When he can look out upon the universe, glorious and terrible, dark and luminous, with a sense of his own littleness in the scheme of things, and yet have faith and courage. When he knows how to make friends and keep them, and above all when he can keep friends with himself. When he can look an honest man or a pure woman straight in the eye. When he loves flowers, can hunt birds without a gun, and can feel the stir of forgotten joy in the laughter of a little child. When he knows that hoeing corn is as honorable as playing golf. When star-crowned trees and the glint of sunlight on flowing waters subdue his soul, like the thought of one much loved and long dead. When he can be happy and high-minded amid the meaner drudgeries of life. When he can look into the face of the most forlorn mortal and see something beside sin. When he knows how to pray. When he is a friend of all good causes and the champion of those who fail. When he can be happy alone. When he has "put away childish things," and yet has kept, through good and evil days, an open mind and a childlike heart. When he has been true to himself, to his fellow man, and to his God—glad to live, but not afraid to die. Such a man is an educated soul, whether he be famous or obscure, rich or poor, high or low.

Orison S. Marden

A person who is enthusiastic soon has enthusiastic followers.

★ ☆ ★ ☆

Try, Try Again

'Tis a lesson you should heed,
Try, try again;
If at first you don't succeed
Try, try again;
Then your courage should persevere,
You will conquer, never fear; Try, try again.
Once or twice though you should fail,
Try, try again;
If you would at last prevail,
Try, try again;
If we strive, 'tis no disgrace
Though we do not win each race;
What should you do in this case? Try, try again.
If you find your task is hard,
Try, try again;
Time will bring you your reward,
Try, try again;
All other folks can do, Why, with patience,
should not you?
Only keep this rule in view, Try, try again!
(From McGuffey's Reader)

★ ☆ ★ ☆

HALF OF BEING SMART IS KNOWING
WHAT YOU'RE DUMB AT.

The best way to better our lot is to do a lot better.

☆ ☆ ☆ ☆ ☆

Commitment to Excellence
By Vince Lombardi

"I owe most everything to football, in which I have spent the greater part of my life. I have never lost my respect, my admiration or my love for what I consider a great game. Each Sunday, after the battle, one group savors victory, another group lives in the bitterness of defeat. The many hurts seem a small price to have paid for having won, and there is no reason at all that is adequate for having lost. To the winner there is one hundred percent fun; and to the loser the only thing left for him is a one hundred percent resolution, one hundred percent determination.

It's a game, I think, a great deal like life in that it demands that a man's personal commitment be toward victory, even though you know that ultimate victory can never be completely won. Yet it must be pursued with all of ones might. Each week there's a new encounter, each year a new challenge. All of the rings and all of the money and all of the color and all of the display linger only in memory. The spirit, the will to win and the will to excel, these are the things that endure and these are the qualities that are so much more important than any of the events that occasion them. I would like to say that the quality of any man's life has got to be full measure of that man's personal commitment to excellence and to victory, regardless of what fields he may be in."

The Saddest Words Of Tongue Or Pen Are These Sad Words...it might have been.

☆ ☆ ☆ ☆ ☆

Enthusiasm!

That certain something that makes us great, that pulls us out of the mediocre and commonplace, that builds into us Power. It glows and shines, it lights up our faces.

Enthusiasm - the keynote that makes us sing and makes men sing with us.

Enthusiasm - the maker of friends, the maker of smiles, the producer of confidence. It cries to the world, "I've got what it takes." It tells all men that our job is a swell job, that the house we work for just suits us fine, the goods we have are the best.

Enthusiasm - the inspiration that makes us "Wake Up and Live." It puts spring in our step, spring in our hearts, a twinkle in our eyes and gives us confidence in ourselves and our fellow man.

Enthusiasm - it changes a dead pan salesman to a producer, a pessimist to an optimist, a loafer to a go-getter.

Enthusiasm - if we have it, we should thank God for it. If we don't have it, then we should get down on our knees and pray for it.

☆ ☆ ☆ ☆ ☆

Upon the plains of hesitation, bleached the bones of countless millions who, on the threshold of victory, sat down to wait, and waiting they died.

A $25,000 IDEA

Ivy Lee once operated an efficiency firm in New York. One day, Lee called on Charles M. Schwab of the Bethlehem Steel Company. Lee outlined briefly his firm's services, ending with the statement, "With our service, you'll know how to manage better." Said Schwab, "I'm not managing as well now as I know how. What we need around here is not more 'knowing' but more 'doing'; not knowledge, but action! If you can give us something to do the things we already know we ought to do, I'll gladly listen to you and pay you anything you ask."

"Fine," said Lee. "I can give you something in twenty minutes that will step up your 'action' and 'doing' at least fifty percent.

Lee pulled a blank card from his pocket, handed it to Schwab and said: "Write on this card the six most important tasks you have to do tomorrow." That took about three minutes. "Now", said Lee, "put this card in your pocket and the first thing tomorrow morning, look at item one and start working on it. Pull the card out of your pocket every fifteen minutes and look at item one until it's finished. Then tackle item two in the same way, then item three. Don't be concerned if you only finish one item. You'll be working on the most important ones. If you can't finish them all by this method, you couldn't with any other method either, and without some system you'd probably not even decide which are the most important.

"Spend the last five minutes of every working day making out a 'must' list for the next day's tasks. After you've convinced yourself of the worth of this system, have your men try it. Try it out as long as you wish and then send me a check for what you think it's worth."

THE PAYOFF...

The whole interview lasted about twentyfive minutes. In two weeks Schwab sent Lee a check for $25,OOO—a thousand dollars a minute. He added a note, saying the lesson was the most profitable from a money standpoint he ever learned. Did it work? In five years it turned the unknown Bethlehem Steel Company into the biggest independent steel producer in the world, made Schwab a hundred million dollar fortune and the best known steel man alive at that time. This idea in various forms has turned more ordinary talents into extraordinary achievements than any article on "Efficiency", "Personality", "Success", or "Psychology", ever heard of. It has made more senior executives out of junior clerks than any complicated system or even a four-year course.

☆ ☆ ☆ ☆ ☆

The Right Angle To Approach Any Problem Is
The TRY Angle.

☆ ☆ ☆ ☆ ☆

We *accomplish* in proportion to what we *attempt.*

You cannot love God without loving every fellow creature He made. An act of contempt or rejection or injustice or neglect toward the least, the lowest, the dumbest, the poorest – is an act against Him. If Christianity does not mean this, it means nothing.

☆ ☆ ☆ ☆ ☆

Believe in Yourself...

   Believe in yourself! Believe you were made to do any task without calling for aid. Believe, without growing too scornfully proud, that you, as the greatest and least, are endowed. A mind to do thinking, two hands and two eyes are all the equipment God gives to the wise. Believe in yourself!
   You're divinely designed and perfectly made for the work of mankind. This truth you must cling to through danger and pain; the heights man has reached you can also attain. Believe to the very last hour, for it's true, that whatever you will you've been gifted to do. Believe in yourself and step out unafraid. By misgivings and doubt be not easily swayed. You've the right to succeed; the precision of skill which betokens the great you can earn if you will! The wisdom of ages is yours if you'll read. But you've got to BELIEVE IN YOURSELF TO **SUCCEED!**

☆ ☆ ☆ ☆ ☆

No dream comes true until you wake up and go to work.

Failure to prepare certainly means preparing to fail.
John Wooden

☆ ☆ ☆ ☆ ☆

MY CREED
By Dean Alfan

I do not choose to be a common man. It is my right to be uncommon...if I can. I seek opportunity - not security. I do not wish to be a kept citizen, humbled and dulled by having the State look after me. I want to take the calculated risk; to dream and to build, to fail and to succeed. I refuse to barter incentive for a dole. I prefer the challenges of life to the guaranteed existence; the thrill of fulfillment to the stale calm of Utopia. I will not trade freedom for beneficence, nor my dignity for a handout. I will never cower before any master or bend to any threat. It is my heritage to stand erect, proud and unafraid; to think and act for myself, enjoy the benefits of my creations, to face the world boldly and say: "This is what I have done."

☆ ☆ ☆ ☆ ☆

TRUST IS THE GREATEST GIFT ONE PERSON CAN GIVE ANOTHER.

COURAGE is what it takes to stand up and speak;
COURAGE is also what it takes to sit down and listen.

☆ ☆ ☆ ☆ ☆

THE MAN IN THE GLASS

When you get what you want in your struggle for self and the world makes you king for a day, just go to the mirror and look at yourself and see what that man has to say. For it isn't your father, mother or wife whose judgement upon you must pass; the fellow whose verdict counts most in your life, is the one staring back from the glass. Some people may think you a straight-shootin' chum and call you a wonderful guy, but the man in the glass says you're only a bum - if you can't look him straight in the eye. He's the fellow to please - never mind all the rest - for he's with you clear up to the end. And you've passed your most dangerous, difficult test if the man in the glass is your friend. You may fool the whole world down the pathway of life and gets pats on your back as you pass. BUT, your final reward will be heartaches and tears - if you've cheated the man in the glass!

☆ ☆ ☆ ☆ ☆

The fellow who never steps on anybody's toes is probably standing still.

When a man has a great deal given to him,
a great deal will be demanded of him.
Luke 12:48

☆ ☆ ☆ ☆ ☆

So You Think You're In A Rut...

Some fellows stay right in the rut while others head the throng. All men may be born equal but - they don't stay that way long. There is many a man with a gallant air, goes galloping to the fray; but the valuable man is the man who's there when the smoke has cleared away. Some "don't get nuthin' out of life" but when their whines begin, we often can remind them that they "don't put nuthin' in."

☆ ☆ ☆ ☆ ☆

IF YOU DON'T HAVE SOME HUMOR WITH PRESSURE, PRESSURE WILL WIN!

☆ ☆ ☆ ☆ ☆

You can't be common. The common goes nowhere. You must be uncommon to be a success in business.

☆ ☆ ☆ ☆ ☆

If a cluttered desk is a sign of a cluttered mind, what's an empty desk the sign of?

TRUE SUCCESS IS OVERCOMING THE FEAR OF BEING UNSUCCESSFUL.

☆ ☆ ☆ ☆ ☆

Tomorrow Never Comes

Tomorrow comes - then it's today so if you have a debt to pay, or work to finish; don't delay.
Tomorrow never comes.
It's fatal to procrastinate, until you find it's just too late, and then to put the blame on fate.
Tomorrow never comes.
The putting right of some mistakes, the gesture that you meant to make, the habit that you vowed to break.
Tomorrow never comes.
So do it now - for fate can play some funny tricks; time slips away; we cannot see beyond today.
Tomorrow never comes.

☆ ☆ ☆ ☆ ☆

THE DIFFERENCE BETWEEN CHAMP AND CHUMP IS "U".

☆ ☆ ☆ ☆ ☆

Following the path of least resistance is what makes men and rivers crooked

TIME CANNOT BE PURCHASED, MARKETED, OR SAVED. IT CAN ONLY BE SPENT. THE SECRET, THEN, IS TO SPEND IT WISELY.

☆ ☆ ☆ ☆ ☆

Advice to Millions Who Rush Through Life:

Take time to think - thoughts are
source of power.
Take time to play - play is the secret of
perpetual youth.
Take time to read - reading is the fountain
of wisdom.
Take time to pray - prayer can be a rock of
strength in time of trouble.
Take time to love - loving is what makes
living worthwhile.
Take time to be friendly - friendships give life
a delicious flavor.
Take time to laugh - laughter is the music
of the soul.
Take time to give - any day of the year is too
short for selfishness.
Take time to do your work well - pride in your
work, no matter what it is, nourishes the
ego and the spirit.
Take time to show appreciation - thanks
is the frosting on the cake of life.

☆ ☆ ☆ ☆ ☆

**PROGRESS COMES FROM
THE INTELLIGENT USE OF EXPERIENCE.**

**We are all MANUFACTURERS --
some make good
others make trouble
and still others make excuses.**

☆ ☆ ☆ ☆ ☆

The great thing in this world is not so much where we are, but in what direction we are moving.
               O.W. Holmes

☆ ☆ ☆ ☆ ☆

If you treat a person as he is, he will remain as he is. If you treat him as though he were what he could be and should be, he will become what he could and should.

☆ ☆ ☆ ☆ ☆

Management maxims:

1. If not controlled, work will flow to the competent personnel until they submerge.
2. The more time you spend in reporting what you're doing, the less time you have to do anything.
          Paul Dickson

☆ ☆ ☆ ☆ ☆

Counting time is not so important as making time count.

Nobody said life would be easy...and you only make it tougher if you feel sorry for yourself.
Morley Fraser

☆ ☆ ☆ ☆ ☆

IT'S UP TO YOU...

You are the fellow that has to decide whether you'll do it or toss it aside. You are the fellow who makes up your mind whether you'll lead or linger behind, whether you'll try for the goal that's afar or be contented to stay where you are. Take it or leave it.

Here's something to do: just think it over, It's all up to you! What do you wish? To be known as a good man who's willing to work, scorned for a loaner or praised by your chief, rich man or poor man or beggar or thief? Eager or earnest or dull through the day, honest or crooked? It's you who must say! You must decide in the face of the test whether you'll shirk it or give it your best.

☆ ☆ ☆ ☆ ☆

A MAN WHO CANNOT LEAD AND WILL NOT FOLLOW INVARIABLY OBSTRUCTS.

☆ ☆ ☆ ☆ ☆

The service we render for others is really the rent we pay for our room on this earth.

KEEP A-GOIN'

Do your darndest when you play,
Keep a-goin'.
To take it easy doesn't pay,
Keep a-goin'.
When the game is pretty tough,
Don't you ever holler "nuff",
Show the world you have the stuff,
Keep a-goin'.
You only need a harder punch,
Keep a-goin'.
'Tain't no use to stand and whine
When they're coming through your line;
Hitch your trousers up and climb,
Keep a-goin'.
If the other team's on top,
Keep a-goin'.
That's just the time you must not stop,
Keep a-goin'.
'S'pose they stop 'most every play;
One good long run may win the day;
To get discouraged doesn't pay,
Keep a-goin'.
When it seems the game is lost,
Keep a-goin'.
Do not stop at any cost
Keep a-goin'.
Don't ever think that you can't win it,
A fightin' team is always in it;

So don't let up a single minute,
Keep a-goin'.

WINNER OR WHINER?

The winner glories in the good; the whiner majors in the mediocre. Winners' thinking processes differ from other peoples'. As part of their normal, moment-to-moment stream of consciousness, winners think constantly in terms of **I can** and **I will.** Losers concentrate their waking thoughts on what they should have done, would have done, what they can't do. When the mind's self-talk is positive, performance is more likely to be successful. The huge majority of our negative doubts and fears are imaginary or beyond our control.
Denis Waitley

☆ ☆ ☆ ☆ ☆

"A father is a thing that is forced to endure childbirth without an anesthetic. A father never feels worthy of the worship in a child's eyes. He's never quite the hero his daughter thinks, never quite the man his son believes him to be, and this worries him sometimes. So he works too hard to try and smooth the rough places in the road for those of his own who will follow him. Fathers are what give daughters away to other men who aren't nearly good enough, so they can have grandchildren who are smarter than anybody's. Fathers make bets with insurance companies about who'll live the longest. One day they lose and the bet's paid off to the part of them they leave behind."
Paul Harvey

BE A THINKER, AND A DREAMER.
BUT MORE IMPORTANT, BE A <u>DOER.</u>

☆ ☆ ☆ ☆ ☆

It's not enough merely to exist. It's not enough to say, "I'm earning enough to live and to support my family. I do my work well. I'm a good father. I'm a good husband. I'm a good churchgoer."

That's all very well. But you must do something more. Seek always to do some good, somewhere. Every man has to seek in his own way to make his own self more noble and to realize his own true worth.

You must give some time to your fellow man. Even if it's a little thing, do something for those who have need of a man's help, something for which you get no pay but the privilege of doing it. For remember, you don't live in a world all your own. Your brothers are here, too.

☆ ☆ ☆ ☆ ☆

To look is one thing.
To see what you look at is another.
To understand what you see is a third.
To learn from what you understand is still something else.
But to act on what you learn is all that really matters, isn't it?
Harvard Business Review

☆ ☆ ☆ ☆ ☆

Constant effort and frequent mistakes are the stepping-stones of genius.

EVERYTHING IS EASIER SAID THAN DONE.

☆ ☆ ☆ ☆

Prudence - the ability to regulate and discipline one's self through the exercise of reason.

Fortitude - the endurance of physical or mental hardships or suffering without giving way under strain. It is firmness of mind in meeting danger or adversity; resolute endurance; courage and staying power. It is the possession of the stamina essential to face that which repels or frightens one, or to put up with the hardships of a job imposed. It implies triumph. Synonyms are grit, backbone, pluck, and guts.

Temperance - habitual moderation in the indulgence of appetites and passions.

Justice - the principle of rectitude and just dealing of men with each other; also conformity to it; integrity.

Faith - trust in God.

Hope - the desire with expectation of obtaining what is desired, or belief that it is obtainable.

Charity - the act of loving all men as brothers because they are sons of God. It stresses benevolence and goodwill in giving and in the broad understanding of others with kindly tolerance.

About all there is to success is making promises and keeping them...

☆ ☆ ☆ ☆ ☆

"I believe my father's overall business philosophy may be accurately summed up in the following tenets he frequently quoted to me when I was young, and which were the principles by which he lived and worked:
• Moral responsibility can never be avoided. The last thing you should ever do is borrow. The first thing you must always do is repay your debts.
• If you can trust a man, a written contract is a waste of paper. If you can't trust him, a written contract is still a waste of paper.
• The man who works for you is entitled to decent wages, decent working conditions and your respect.
• Money is only as good as what you do with it. The best thing you can do with your money is to keep it working to produce more and better goods and services for more people at lower prices."

J. Paul Getty

☆ ☆ ☆ ☆ ☆

YOU ONLY LIVE ONCE - IF YOU DO IT RIGHT ONCE IS ENOUGH!

TACT IS THE ART OF MAKING A POINT WITHOUT MAKING AN ENEMY.

☆ ☆ ☆ ☆ ☆

Hardening of the heart ages people more quickly than hardening of the arteries.

☆ ☆ ☆ ☆ ☆

Every human being - for vitality, maturity, growth, and fulfillment - needs constant stress and constant risk in order to reach his fullness as a creature. When you play it safe - as so many are trying to do - and get a job and bury yourself in the soft, amorphous womb of industry or some giant corporation, quite often you begin to lose the qualities that make a human being great or successful. You tend to relax; you tend to **stop growing.**
    Earl Nightingale

☆ ☆ ☆ ☆ ☆

BE A SELF-STARTER AND YOUR BOSS WON'T HAVE TO BE A CRANK.

☆ ☆ ☆ ☆ ☆

Enthusiasm without knowledge is like running in the dark.

Courage consists not in blindly overlooking danger, but in seeing it and conquering.

☆ ☆ ☆ ☆ ☆

RESOLUTIONS

No one will get out of this world alive. Resolve therefore in the year to maintain a sense of values. Take care of yourself. Good health is everyone's major source of wealth. Without it, happiness is almost impossible. Resolve to be cheerful and helpful. Avoid angry, abrasive persons. They are generally vengeful. Avoid zealots. They are generally humorless. Resolve to listen more and talk less. No one ever learns anything by talking. Be leery of giving advice. Wise men don't need it, and fools won't heed it. Resolve to be tender with the young, compassionate with the aged, sympathetic with the striving and tolerant of the weak and the wrong. Sometimes in life you will have been all of these. Do not equate money with success. There are many successful money-makers who are miserable failures as human beings. What counts most about success is how a man achieves it. Resolve to love - next year - someone you didn't love this year. Love is the most enriching ingredient of life.

☆ ☆ ☆ ☆ ☆

A leader is best when people barely know he exists. When his work is done, his aim fulfilled, they will say, "We did this ourselves".

"I must do something" will always solve more problems than "Something must be done."

☆ ☆ ☆ ☆ ☆

"Do the very best you can with what you have."
T. Roosevelt

☆ ☆ ☆ ☆ ☆

When you're ready to quit and to give up the fight, and the skies all above you are black as the night, then lift up your hand and through the owly night air, there is power and triumph in confident prayer.

☆ ☆ ☆ ☆ ☆

HE WHO WON'T BE DENIED WILL FIND A WAY.

☆ ☆ ☆ ☆ ☆

Independence is God given - **be thankful**
Fame is man given - **be humble**
Conceit is self given - **be careful**

☆ ☆ ☆ ☆ ☆

THE BIGGER A MAN'S HEAD GETS, THE EASIER IT IS TO FILL HIS SHOES.

Pride...Character...Work Habits...
LEAD TO SUCCESS!
Rick Comley

☆ ☆ ☆ ☆ ☆

Been Criticized Lately?

"It is not the critic who counts, nor the man who points out how the strong man stumbled, or where the doer of deeds could have done them better. The credit belongs to the man who was actually in the arena; whose fate is marred by dust and sweat and blood; who errs and comes short again; who knows the great enthusiasms, the great devotions, and spends himself in a worthy cause; who at best knows in the end the triumph of high achievement; and at worst, if he fails, at least while daring greatly; so that his pace shall never be with those cold and timid souls who know neither victory or defeat."

Theodore Roosevelt

☆ ☆ ☆ ☆ ☆

THE MEASURE OF A MAN'S REAL CHARACTER IS WHAT HE WOULD DO IF HE KNEW HE NEVER WOULD BE FOUND OUT.

T.B. Macaulay

☆ ☆ ☆ ☆ ☆

In Business...
The person who gets ahead is the one who does more than is necessary and keeps on doing it.

A salesman always kept his hat on while doing "desk work" at the office. When kidded about it, he answered, "That's to remind me I really ought not be here." (American Salesman)

☆ ☆ ☆ ☆

THE ONLY WAY TO WIN

It takes a little courage
And a little self-control,
And some grim determination,
If you want to reach your goal.
It takes a deal of striving,
And a firm and stern-set chin,
No matter what the battle,
If you really want to win.

There's no easy path to glory,
There's no rosy road to fame.
Life, however we may view it,
Is no simple parlor game;
But its prizes call for fighting,
For endurance and for grit;
For a rugged disposition
And a don't-know-when-to-quit.

You must take a blow or give one,
You must risk and you must lose,
And expect that in the struggle,
You will suffer from the bruise.
But you must not wince or falter,
If a fight you once begin;
Be a man and face the battle
That's the only way to win.

A MAN'S HAPPINESS AND SUCCESS IN LIFE WILL DEPEND NOT SO MUCH UPON WHAT HE HAS OR UPON WHAT POSITION HE OCCUPIES AS UPON WHAT HE *IS*, AND THE HEART HE CARRIES INTO HIS POSITION.
J.J. WILSON

☆ ☆ ☆ ☆ ☆

The royal road to success would have more travelers if so many weren't lost attempting to find short cuts.
H.C. Calvin

☆ ☆ ☆ ☆ ☆

There is a four-word formula for success that applies equally well to organization or individuals: make yourself more useful.

☆ ☆ ☆ ☆ ☆

IF YOU HAVE TRIED TO DO SOMETHING AND FAILED, YOU ARE VASTLY BETTER OFF THAN IF YOU HAD TRIED TO DO NOTHING AND SUCCEEDED.

☆ ☆ ☆ ☆ ☆

There are few, if any, jobs in which ability alone is sufficient. Needed also are loyalty, sincerity, enthusiasm and cooperation.

A SUCCESSFUL PERSON IS ONE WHO WENT AHEAD AND DID THE THING THE REST OF US NEVER QUITE GOT AROUND TO.

☆ ☆ ☆ ☆ ☆

STICK IT OUT

When your world's about to fall, and your back's against the wall, when you're facing wild retreat and utter rout; when it seems that naught can stop it, all your pleas and plans can't prop it, get a grip upon yourself and - **stick it out!**

Any craven fool can quit, but a man with pluck and grit will hold until the very final shout; in the snarling teeth of sorrow he will laugh and say "Tomorrow the luck will change, I guess I'll stick it out."

The luck does change - you know it - all the records prove and show it, and the men who win are men who strangle doubt, don't hesitate nor swerve, who have grit and guts and nerve, and whose motto is: work hard, and **stick it out.**

And you think you can't last long, so you, when things go wrong, that you've got to quit nor wait for the final bout; smile, smile at your beholders, clench your teeth and square your shoulders and fight! You'll win if you but **STICK IT OUT!!**

☆ ☆ ☆ ☆ ☆

It ain't braggin' if you've done it.

When you affirm big, believe big and pray big, big things happen.
Norman Vincent Peale

☆ ☆ ☆ ☆ ☆

CLIMB 'TIL YOUR DREAM COMES TRUE
Often your tasks will be many, and more than you think you can do. Often the road will be rugged and the hills insurmountable, too. But always remember, the hills ahead are never as steep as they seem, and with faith in your heart start upward and climb 'til you reach your dream. For nothing in life that is worthy is ever too hard to achieve if you have the courage to try it and you have the faith to believe, for faith is a force that is greater than knowledge or power or skill, and many defeats turn to triumph if you trust in God's wisdom and will. For faith is a mover of mountains - there's nothing that God cannot do - so start today with faith in your heart and **CLIMB 'TIL YOUR DREAMS COME TRUE!**

☆ ☆ ☆ ☆ ☆

Make a good rule, and pray God to help you to keep it. Never, if possible, lie down at night without being able to say: I have made one human being, at least, a little wiser, a little happier, or a little better this day.
> Charles Kingsley

Duties delayed are the devil's delight.

☆ ☆ ☆ ☆ ☆

It might be just as offensive to be around a man who never changed his mind as one who never changed his clothes.

☆ ☆ ☆ ☆ ☆

SO YOU FEEL YOU'RE IN A RUT
Some fellows stay right in the rut while others head the throng. All men may be born equal - but they don't stay that way long. There is many a man with a gallant air, goes galloping to the fray; but the valuable man is the man who's there when the smoke has cleared away. Some say "I don't get nuthin' out of life" but when their whines begin, we often can remind them that they "Don't put nuthin' in."

☆ ☆ ☆ ☆ ☆

INGENUITY, PLUS COURAGE, PLUS WORK EQUALS MIRACLES.
    Rev. Bob Richards

☆ ☆ ☆ ☆ ☆

BE KIND. REMEMBER EVERYONE YOU MEET IS FIGHTING A HARD BATTLE.

**Silence is not always golden...
sometimes it is just plain yellow.**

☆ ☆ ☆ ☆ ☆

Dykes of Courage

Courage and cowardice are antithetical.
Courage is an inner resolution to go forward in spite of obstacles and frightening situations; cowardice is a submissive surrender to circumstance.
Courage breeds creative self-affirmation; cowardice produces destructive self-abnegation.
Courage faces fear and thereby masters it; cowardice represses fear and is thereby mastered by it.
Courageous men never lose the zest for living even though their life situation is zestless; cowardly men, overwhelmed by the uncertainties of life, lose the will to live.
We must constantly build dykes of courage to hold back the flood of fear.

Martin Luther King, Jr.

☆ ☆ ☆ ☆ ☆

Temper is what gets most of us in trouble. Pride is what keeps us there.

☆ ☆ ☆ ☆ ☆

Some people are so indecisive their favorite color is plaid.

Character is a conquest, not a bequest.

☆ ☆ ☆ ☆ ☆

MY DAD
By Mamie Ozbun Odum

You have been a mighty dandy pal,
You held my baby hand,
You soothed away imagined hurts;
Helped me on my feet to stand.

You always knew each childish want,
And chased away my fears,
Encouraged me when things went wrong,
And wiped away my tears.

Yes, Dad, you walked each day with me.
When the pace was hard and long,
Undying courage you instilled,
Teaching right, condemning wrong.

You father - wisdom daily gave.
New courage to my heart,
Never tiring, just standing by,
Quietly doing your part.
When now we meet at manhood's gate,
You're the best pal I ever had,
You'll never know what you mean to me,
As I so simply say,
"Thanks, Dad!"

Good, Better, Best. Never let it rest, 'til your Good is Better, and your Better is BEST.

☆ ☆ ☆ ☆ ☆

TOMORROW'S OPPORTUNITY

If we might have a second chance
To live the days once more
And rectify mistakes we've made
To even up the score.

If we might have a second chance
To use the knowledge gained
Perhaps we might become at last
As fine as God ordained.

But though we can't retrace our steps,
However stands the score,
Tomorrow brings another chance
For us to try once more.
— Hilda Butler Farr

☆ ☆ ☆ ☆ ☆

THE TROUBLE WITH THE WORLD IS NOT THAT PEOPLE KNOW TOO LITTLE, BUT THAT THEY KNOW SO MANY THINGS THAT AIN'T SO.

☆ ☆ ☆ ☆ ☆

Mistrust the man who finds everything good, the man who finds everything evil, and still more, the man who is indifferent to everything.

There is no security in this life, only opportunity.

Gen. Douglas MacArthur

☆ ☆ ☆ ☆ ☆

No one has a right to live in idleness and expect to live long and be happy. The ship anchored in the harbor rots faster than the ship crossing the ocean; a still pond of water stagnates more rapidly than a running stream. Our unused minds are subject to atrophy much more rapidly than those in use. The unused cells in our brains deteriorate much faster than those which are continually exercised. Hence, to remain young we must remain active.

☆ ☆ ☆ ☆ ☆

THERE IS NO RIGHT WAY TO DO THE WRONG THING.

☆ ☆ ☆ ☆ ☆

The sales manager told his crew, "You fellows don't make enough calls. If you'd make more calls, you'd sell more merchandise."
At the next sales meeting one bright young fellow raised his hand and said, "I made 47 calls yesterday."
"That's fine," said the sales manager. "I commend you."
"I would have made more," the young man continued, "but some fool stopped me and asked what I was selling."

Leo Aikman

A leader must have courage to make a decision and stick with it knowing that people are going to criticize you no matter what you do.

☆ ☆ ☆ ☆

The world stands aside to let anyone pass who knows where he is going.
Jordan

☆ ☆ ☆ ☆

What Are You Doing Now?

It matters not if you lost the fight and were
badly beaten too.
It matters not if you failed outright in the things you
tried to do. It matters not if you toppled down from
the azure heights of blue,
But what are you doing now????
It matters not if your plans were foiled and
your hopes have fallen through.
It matters not if your chance was spoiled for the
gain almost in view.
It matters not if you missed the goal though you
struggled brave and true...
But what are you doing now????
It matters not if your fortune's gone and your fame
has vanished too.
It matters not if a cruel world's score be directed
straight at you.
It matters not if the worst has come and your dreams
have not come true...
But what are you doing now????
R. Rhodes Stabley

ARE YOU STRONG ENOUGH TO HANDLE SUCCESS?

Unfortunately, the road to anywhere is filled with many pitfalls, and it takes a man of determination and character not to fall into them. As I have said many times, whenever you get your head above the average, someone will be there to take a poke at you. That is to be expected in any phase of life. However, as I have also said many times before, if you see a man on top of a mountain, he didn't just light there! Chances are he had to climb through many difficulties and with a great expenditure of energy in order to get there, and the same is true of a man in any profession; be he a great attorney, a great minister, a great man of medicine or a great businessman. I am certain he worked with a definite plan and an aim and purpose in life. I have always thought that an excerpt from Parkenham Beatty's "Self Reliance" contained a good philosophy for each coach:

> *"By your own soul learn to live, and if men thwart you, take no heed, if men hate you, have no care; Sing your song, dream your dream, hope your hope and pray your prayer."*

I am sure that if a coach will follow this philosophy of life, he will be successful. To set by and worry about criticism, which too often comes from the misinformed or from those incapable of passing judgement on an individual or a problem, is a waste of time.

–Adolph Rupp
Former University of Kentucky Basketball Coach, Record High 874 Career Victories.

A lot of people love their jobs. It's the work they hate.

☆ ☆ ☆ ☆ ☆

$UCCESS

What is the price of success? It is simply:

To use all of your courage to force yourself to concentrate on the problem at hand, to think of it deeply and constantly, to study it from all angles, and to plan.

To have a high and sustained determination to put over what you plan to accomplish, no matter what circumstances may arise, and nothing worthwhile has ever been accomplished without some obstacles overcome.

To refuse to believe that there are any circumstances sufficiently strong to defeat you in the accomplishment of your purpose.

HARD?! I should say so! That's why so many men never attempt to acquire success. They answer the siren call of the rut, and remain on the beaten paths for beaten men. Nothing worthwhile has ever been achieved without constant endeavor, some pain, and constant application of the lash of ambition. That's the price of success.

Every man should ask himself: Am I willing to endure the pain of this struggle for the comforts and the rewards and the glory that go with achievement? Or shall I accept the uneasy and inadequate contentment that comes with mediocrity? **Am I willing to pay the price of success?**

IF YOU KNOW IT, SHOW IT!

☆ ☆ ☆ ☆ ☆

THE TEN COMMANDMENTS OF HUMAN RELATIONS

1. Speak to people. There's nothing as nice as a cheerful greeting.
2. Smile at people. It takes 72 muscles to frown and only 14 to smile.
3. Call people by their name. The sweetest music to the ears is one's own name.
4. Be friendly and helpful. If you would have friends, be friendly.
5. Be cordial. Speak and act as if every thing you did were a pleasure.
6. Be genuinely interested in people.
7. Be generous with praise, cautious with criticism.
8. Be considerate with the feelings of others; it will be appreciated.
9. Be thoughtful of others opinions. There are three sides to every controversy yours, the others - and the right one.
10. Be alert to give service. What counts a great deal in life is what we do for others.

☆ ☆ ☆ ☆ ☆

TO GET THE TRUE MEASURE OF A MAN, NOTE HOW MUCH MORE HE DOES THAN IS REQUIRED OF HIM.

**COUNT YOUR LIFE BY SMILES
NOT TEARS.
COUNT YOUR AGE BY FRIENDS
NOT YEARS.**

☆ ☆ ☆ ☆ ☆

A LITTLE HISTORY LESSON

In his Decline and Fall of the Roman Empire, which he wrote in 1788, Edward Gibbon defined five basic reasons why that civilization withered and died. One wonders whether historians centuries from now will find a deadly parallel between the U.S. and Imperial Rome. Here are the flaws that Gibbon detected:
1. An undermining of the dignity and sanctity of the home, which is the basis for human society.
2. Higher and higher taxes, and spending public money for free bread and circuses for the populace.
3. A mad craze for pleasure, with pastimes becoming every year more exciting, brutal, and immoral.
4. Building great armaments, although the real enemy was within, the decay of individual responsibility.
5. Decay of religion - faith fading into mere form, losing touch with life and losing power to guide the people.

☆ ☆ ☆ ☆ ☆

IT IS MORE IMPORTANT TO KNOW WHERE YOU ARE GOING THAN TO GET THERE QUICKLY.
M. Newcomber

Trouble is a great sieve through which we sift our acquaintances: those who are too big to pass through are friends.

☆ ☆ ☆ ☆ ☆

PLAYING THE GAME

So you played the game, and you lost, my lad? And you're battered and bleeding too. And your hopes are dead and your heart is lead. And your whole world's sad and blue. And you sob and cry in your grief and your pain for the hopes that had to die. But the game is through and it's up to you to laugh, though you want to cry. For someone there must lose, my lad it's sad but it's always true. And day by day in the games you play it's sure sometimes to be you. So grit your teeth to the pain, my lad for you battled the best you could. And there's never shame, in the losing game when you lose like a real man should. For after all, life is a game, my lad, and we play it as best we may. We win or lose as the gods may choose, who govern the games we play. But whether we win or lose, my lad, at the end when the battle's through, we must wait with a smile for the after while and the chances that will come anew...

☆ ☆ ☆ ☆ ☆

TOUGH TIMES NEVER LAST, TOUGH PEOPLE DO.

"Things Are Never Quite So Bad As We Imagine"

Keep up a brave spirit; things are never quite so bad as we imagine they may be. God always lets in the sunshine somewhere. Hope on; no matter how dark the way seems, it is better farther on. Do not be discouraged; if business is dull, if troubles overwhelm you, if you have losses and crosses, or if you are deceived and disappointed, go on hoping and trusting; there is a good time coming for you!

Take hold of the every-day duties, and if they are not to your taste and of your seeking, honor them anyway. By doing these things well, you shall be found worthy of greater ones.

Work and hope; your Better Day will dawn.

☆ ☆ ☆ ☆ ☆

The Man Who Sulks

The world has little pity and few favors to be spent for the man who is disgruntled and sits sulking in his tent; if your ventures have not prospered do not idly curse your luck, but get out and make the people wonder at your manly pluck. Men will never come to coax you, if you hang back in despair, to have courage and keep trying to put off the frown you wear; they will not arrange new chances to replace the ones you lose while you haunt a gloomy corner clinging to a case of blues. They are foolishly self-cheated who keep harping on their woes after they have been defeated, thinking all men are their foes, and the praise the world is willing to bestow is never meant for the man who is disgruntled and sits sulking in his tent.

THREE WORDS OF STRENGTH
by Schiller

There are three lessons I would write, three words, as with a burning pen, in tracings of eternal light, upon the hearts of men.

Have hope. Though clouds environ round and gladness hides her face in scorn, put off the shadow from thy brow; no night but hath its morn.

Have faith. Where'er thy bark is driven the calm's disport, the tempest's mirth know this: God rules the hosts of heaven, the inhabitants of earth.

Have love. Not love alone for one, but man, as man, thy brother call; and scatter, like a circling sun, thy charities on all.

☆ ☆ ☆ ☆ ☆

Never leave business to look for business. Do today's business today and tomorrow's business tomorrow.

☆ ☆ ☆ ☆ ☆

DREAMS
by Langston Hughes

Hold fast to dreams for if dreams die, life is a broken-winged bird that cannot fly. Hold fast to dreams for when dreams go, life is a barren field frozen with snow.

Twenty-one Maxims for Better Living
by George Washington

1. Sleep not when others speak, sit not when others stand, speak not when you should hold your peace, and walk not when others stop.

2. Let your discourse with men of business be short and comprehensive.

3. In writing or speaking, give to every person his due title, according to his degree and the custom of the place.

4. Strive not with your superiors in argument, but always submit your judgment to others with modesty.

5. When about to advise or reprehend any one, consider whether it ought to be in public or private, presently or at some other time; also in what terms to do it; and in reproving, show no signs of choler, but do it with sweetness and mildness.

6. Take all admonitions thankfully, in whatsoever place given; but afterwards, not being culpable, take a time or place convenient to let him know it that gave them.

7. Be not hasty to believe belying reports, to the disparagement of any one.

8. Associate yourself with men of good quality if you esteem your own reputation, for it is better to be alone than in bad company.

9. Let your conversation be without malice or envy, for it is a sign of a tractable and commendable nature, and in all cases of passion admit reason to govern.

10. Speak not injurious words neither in jest or in earnest. Scoff at none, although they give occasion.

11. Detract not from others, but neither be excessive in commending.

12. If two contend together, take not the part of either unconstrained, and be not obstinate in your opinion; in things indifferent be of the major side.

13. When another speaks, be attentive yourself, and disturb not the audience. If any hesitate in his words help him not, and answer him not till his speech be ended.

14. Undertake not what you cannot perform, but be careful to keep your promise.

15. In disputes, be not so desirous to overcome that you do not give liberty to each one to deliver his opinion, and submit to the judgment of the major part especially if they are judges of the dispute.

16. Be not tedious in discourse, make not many digressions, nor repeat often the same matter of discourse.

17. Speak no evil of the absent, for it is unjust.

18. Be not angry at the table whatever happens, and if you have reason to be so, show it not; put on a cheerful countenance, especially if there be strangers, for good humor makes one dish a feast.

19. Seat not yourself at the upper end of the table, but if it be your due or the master of the house will have it so, contend not lest you should trouble the company.

20. Let your recreations be manful, not sinful.

21. Labor to keep alive your breast the little spark of celestial fire called conscience.

The metal of man's soul was made to ring, not to whine.

✩ ✩ ✩ ✩ ✩

COMFORT

Say! You've struck a heap of trouble, bust in business, lost your wife; no one cares a cent about you, you don't care a cent for life; hard luck has of hope bereft you, health is failing, wish you'd die - why, you've still the sunshine left you and the big, blue sky.

Sky so blue it makes you wonder if it's heaven shining through; earth so smiling 'way out yonder, sun so bright it dazzles you; birds a-singing, flowers a-flinging all their fragrance on the breeze; dancing shadows, green, still meadows - don't you mope, you've still got these.

These, and none can take them from you; these, and none can weigh their worth. What! you're tired and broke and beaten? Why, you're rich - you've got the earth! Yes, if you're a tramp in tatters, while the blue sky bends above you've got nearly all that matters - you've got God, and God is love.

Robert W. Service

✩ ✩ ✩ ✩ ✩

If you will succeed in life's business, do what you ought to do when you ought to do it, whether you want to or not.

Why can't somebody give us a list of things that everybody thinks and nobody says, and another list of things that everybody says and nobody thinks?

☆ ☆ ☆ ☆ ☆

What Is Success?
To laugh often and love much;
To win the respect of intelligent persons and
the affection of children;
To earn the approval of honest critics and endure
the betrayal of false friends;

To appreciate beauty;
To find the best in others;
To give of one's self without the slightest
thought of return;
To have accomplished a task, whether by a
healthy child, a rescued soul, a garden patch or a
redeemed social condition;
To have played and laughed with enthusiasm
and sung with exaltation;

To know that even one life has breathed
easier because you have lived;
This is to have succeeded.
-Anonymous

☆ ☆ ☆ ☆ ☆

Organization without cooperation is like a fiddle with one string - some notes, but not much music.

Ten Short Hints for...

1. Pursue the business you are engaged in with zeal and avidity. Without much industry and energy, your time will melt away with little or no profit. It follows from this obvious rule that you ought to concentrate your attention upon one particular line of business, rather than distract it among several.

2. Mind your own concerns; do not trust implicitly to agents or clerks. If you wish anything well done, you must either do it yourself, or see it done by others. Even your agent will soon learn to despise you, as well as neglect your concerns, unless you show an interest in them yourself. Attend to your business, and he will attend to it. Neglect it yourself, your agent will neglect it. If he does not, take that man to your heart; he is one man out of ten thousand.

3. It naturally flows from the last rule that you must rise early to see the course of your business. The man who wastes the first moments of the day in bed is sure to produce the same habit among all those who live within the range of his influence.

4. In all cases prefer your business to your pleasures. The former not only suffers from your neglect, but your reputation as a man of punctuality and industry suffers with it.

5. Let your credit always keep pace with your capital. Never stretch it but on some great emergency, lest you snap it. Let the world see that you would rather make slow and sure gains than venture some risks.

...Men of Business 1830

6. When you are under the necessity of appealing to your friends, you ought never to ask it, unless you in your turn incur an equal responsibility for them, or make them secure by a pledge of property.

7. Make no important agreement unless you reduce it to writing. Men may prove scoundrels; or their memories, at least, may prove treacherous. The ink will remain as it is; but words, volatile words will fly away and be forgotten.

8. Observe the utmost order in the prosecution of your business. Enter every debt or credit as it occurs. Beware of the foul fiend Ennui, and mind the good maxim "to do everything while you think of it." Have a place for everything, and let everything be in its place - more especially your papers, for more is lost and vexation incurred by a hunt after some straggling document, than is generally conceived.

9. Take a receipt for all monies you pay, or any debts, in whatever way you discharge them. These receipts must not be taken on loose bits of paper which may be mislaid from their place, or lost from their file for what injury may not arise from their loss? To remedy this inconvenience, I earnestly advise you to have a large blank book set apart for the purpose of registering your receipts.

10. As nearly as possible, settle your accounts at least once a year.

The great trouble with the school of experience is that the course is so long that the graduates are too old to go to work.

☆ ☆ ☆ ☆ ☆

Some Success Factors In Business

Keep your business to yourself. Listen more and talk less. Be particular about your personal appearance. Be particular about your social contacts. Don't be a "yes" man. Speak your mind freely if you think someone else is wrong. Ambition, determination and persistence are the foundations of success. Success is a state of mind; attitude is the rudder that gets you to the objective. Build up as large a circle of good friends as possible. The best way to have a friend is to be a friend. Do not indulge in anything to excess. Exercise regularly, look after your health. In later years, when middle age begins to creep upon you, keep your contact with the youth of your community. It will keep you young in spirit. Be prompt. Do not be the last one to report for work and do not be the first one to leave. Do not be afraid to make mistakes, but if you do, admit them and try to profit by them.

The Ten Demandments

Back in the early days of the Industrial Revolution, a London factory manager compiled a list of advice that he passed along to his employees. Here are his "Ten Demandments".

1. Don't lie. It wastes my time and yours. I am sure to catch you in the end.

2. Watch your work, not the clock. A long day's work makes a long day short and a short day's work makes my face long.

3. Give me more than I expect, and I will give you more than you expect.

4. You owe so much to yourself that you cannot afford to owe anybody else.

5. Dishonesty is never an accident. Good men, like good women, never see temptation when they meet it.

6. Mind your own business, and in time you'll have a business of your own to mind.

7. Don't be anything here which hurts your self-respect. An employee who is willing to steal for me is willing to steal from me.

8. It is none of my business what you do at night. But if dissipation affects what you do the next day, and you do half as much as I demand, you'll last half as long as you hoped.

9. Don't tell me what I'd like to hear, but what I ought to hear. I don't want a valet to my vanity, but one for my money.

10. Don't kick if I kick. If you're worth correcting, you're worth keeping. I don't waste time cutting specks out of rotten apples.

TEN THINGS I LEARNED IN A HALF CENTURY OF LIVING

1. A man who wants time to read and write must let the grass grow long.
2. The hardest part of raising children is teaching them to ride bicycles. A father can either run beside the bicycle or stand yelling directions while the child falls.
3. It's impossible to treat a child too well. Children are spoiled by being ignored too much or by harshness, not by kindness.
4. It is impossible to treat a woman too well.
5. The definition of a beautiful woman is one who loves me.
6. Children go away and live their own lives, starting when they are about 18. Parents who accept this as a natural part of the order of things will see their grown children surprisingly often.
7. Success in almost any field depends more on energy and drive than it does on intelligence. This explains why we have so many stupid leaders.
8. When things break around the house, call a handyman. No intelligent man is capable of fixing anything.
9. Either afloat or ashore, it is normal for everything to go wrong. No one should ever be surprised or unduly upset by foul-ups. They are a basic part of the human condition.
10. When I was young I was briefly interested in politics, but politics soon bored me. I was interested in business for a long while, but business eventually bored me. Although it may sound sentimental, the only real meaning I have found in life has been in my wife and children. Without them, I would be in more despair than a bankrupt millionaire.

Never try to make anyone like yourself. You know, and God knows, that one of you is enough.
Ralph Waldo Emerson

☆ ☆ ☆ ☆ ☆

WHO PROFITS THE MOST FOR THE COUNTRY?
(Who profits most from profit?)
• Did the Liberals save millions of American women from back-breaking work by inventing the vacuum cleaner and washing machine-or was it businessmen looking for profit?
• Did union leaders create modern life-giving drugs, or was it businesses in search of profit?
• Is it government bureaucracy or profit seeking corporations which generate the millions of American jobs paying the highest wages in the world?
• Was it the Welfare State or men who wanted to become millionaires who developed the automobiles and the hundreds of thousands of jobs which followed?
• When those who criticize and attack profit can equal this record for their country, it will be time to listen to them...
       ...But not until.

☆ ☆ ☆ ☆ ☆

If you blame others for your failures, do you credit others with your successes?

Little Prizes

Most of us miss out on life's big prizes: the Pulitzer, the Nobel, the Oscars, Tonys and Emmys.

But we're all eligible for life's small pleasures. A pat on the back. A kiss behind the ear. A four-pound bass. A full moon. An empty parking space. A crackling fire. A great meal. A glorious sunset.

Don't fret about copping life's grand awards. Enjoy its tiny delights. There are plenty for all of us.

☆ ☆ ☆ ☆ ☆

Someone has calculated how a typical lifespan of 70 years is spent. Here is his estimate:

Sleep	23 years	32.9%
Work	16 years	22.8%
TV	8 years	11.4%
Eating	6 years	8.6%
Travel	6 years	8.6%
Leisure	42 years	6.5%
Illness	4 years	5.7%
Dressing	2 years	2.8%
Religion	1/2 year	0.7%
TOTAL	**70 years**	**100.%**

☆ ☆ ☆ ☆ ☆

SOME THINK THEY HAVE MADE A SUCCESS OF LIFE, WHEN ALL THEY'VE MADE IS JUST A LOT OF MONEY.

David Ogilvy's Philosophy of Advertising:
"Never write an advertisement which you wouldn't want your own family to read. You wouldn't tell lies to your own wife. Don't tell them to mine. Do as you would be done by. If you tell lies about a product, you will be found out - either by the Government, which will prosecute you, or by the consumer who will punish you by not buying your product a second time. Good products can be sold by honest advertising. If you don't think the product is good, you have no business advertising it."

☆ ☆ ☆ ☆ ☆

Dear Ann Landers: I thought you'd like to know how I have applied your good common - sense advice to my business.

Often, a woman who is contemplating marriage writes to say she is worried because her fiance treats her badly and may even slap her around. She asks, "Do you believe he will treat me better once we're married? He says he will." Your reply is, "No. He will treat you worse. Before marriage his best foot is forward. After marriage, you will see a less attractive side."

As a buyer, I am often called on by sales representatives who are trying to get my business on a steady basis. I listen to the pitch, and if it's good, I apply the Ann Landers Test: I give an assignment, such as obtaining specific detailed information from the factory. Some of these representatives fail to follow through or do so halfheartedly. A few get back to me promptly with exactly what was requested and sometimes more.

I reason that if a sales representative doesn't follow through when he's trying to get my business, he sure won't do better once I'm signed up and "married" to him.
A.H.S., St. Louis

Dear Saint: Behavioral and character traits that one displays in personal relationships are bound to carry over in business situations. I'm glad I was helpful.

STRESS:

The confusion created when one's mind overrides the body's basic desire to choke the living hell out of some jerk who desperately needs it!!!

☆ ☆ ☆ ☆ ☆

The company he chooses...

It was sometime in November,
In a town I can't remember.
I was carrying home a jug with
maudlin' pride.
When my feet began to stutter
and I fell down in the gutter
And a pig came up and lay down by
my side.

As I lay there in the gutter
Thinking thoughts I dared not utter,
A lady passing by was heard to say,
"You can tell a man who boozes
by the company he chooses,"
And the pig got up and slowly
walked away.

Moral: Pick your friends & associates with care.

What is a Customer?

A Customer is the most important person ever in this office . . . in person or by mail.

A Customer is not dependent on us . . . we are dependent on him.

A Customer is not an interruption of our work . . . he is the purpose of it. We are not doing him a favor by serving him . . .he is doing us a favor by giving us the opportunity to do so.

A Customer is not an outsider to our business . . . he is a part of it.

A Customer is not a cold statistic . . . he is a flesh-and-blood human being with feelings and emotions like your own, and with biases and prejudices.

A Customer is not someone to argue or match wits with. Nobody ever won an argument with a customer.

A Customer is a person who brings us his wants. It is our job to handle them profitably to him and to ourselves.

Author Unknown

The Lowest Bidder

It's unwise to pay too much, but it is worse to pay too little. When you pay too much, you lose a little money—that is all. When you pay too little, you sometimes lose everything, because the thing you bought was incapable of doing the thing it was bought to do. The common law of business-balance prohibits paying a little and getting a lot—it can't be done. If you deal with the lowest bidder, it is well to add something for the risk you run. And if you do that, you will have enough to pay for something better.

John Ruskin (1819-1900)

☆ ☆ ☆ ☆ ☆

God is good, God is fair. To some he gave brains, to others hair.

☆ ☆ ☆ ☆ ☆

Begin with yourself...

"There's only one corner of the universe you can be certain of improving, and that's your own self. So you have to begin there . . . not outside, not with other people. That comes afterward—when you've worked on your own corner. You've got to be good before you can do good."   — Aldous Huxley

What is success?

All too often in this materialistic world, we judge "success" as how much money someone makes or how much wealth one has accumulated.

Success—true success—has to be more encompassing than just a six-figure income. Perhaps a definition of success should not include a monetary figure at all. For one man's success as a teacher definitely is not going to earn him big bucks in comparison to the man who is a success as a movie actor.

One of Webster's definitions of "success" is "the attainment of wealth, favor or eminence." It does not mention, however, what kind of wealth, whose favor, or in whose eyes this eminence must be gained.

It is like asking "Who is smarter, men or women?" You cannot answer because you do not know what criteria are involved with making the judgment.

Success in business is usually measured in how much money one makes. But the personal success of a businessman may be for him that he has done a good job, made a good product, and in some cases just kept his job for 25 years.

Success, like beauty, is in the eye of the beholder! It is a judgment call. The statement, "He's a success in everything he does," sounds like there is no other way to look at it—he is a success! But, how does he feel about it? If his "successes" in others' eyes have not gained him the self-fulfillment he wants, then he is no success in his own eyes.

On the other hand, there are people who say, "Poor Joe! Same job, same company, for all these years." But Joe sees himself as highly productive, doing that one job better than anyone else, and asks no more than to be left to do that job the best way he can. He is a success in his own eyes.

Success is sometimes considered synonymous with "effect." A man is happy if he influences the lives, works and attitudes of his fellow man... he is a success. The happiest people seem to be those who have been able to improve the state of someone else's being.

Perhaps, then, success is attaining happiness ... whatever that may be for you.

THE BUSY MAN

If you want to get a favor done
   By some obliging friend
And want a promise, safe and sure,
   On which you may depend,
Don't go to him who always has
   Much leisure time to plan
But if you want your favor done,
   Just ask the busy man.
The man with leisure never has
   A moment he can spare,
He's always "putting off" until
   His friends are in despair.
But he whose every waking hour
   Is crowded full of work,
Forgets the art of wasting time,
   He cannot stop to shirk.
So when you want a favor done
   And want it right away,
Go to the man who constantly
   Works twenty hours a day.
He'll find a moment sure, somewhere,
   That has no other use,
And fix you while the idle man
     Is framing an excuse.

☆ ☆ ☆ ☆ ☆

Marshall Field, American business leader and philanthropist, said, "Those who enter to buy support me. Those who come to flatter please me. Those who complain teach me how I may please others so that more will come. Only those hurt me who are displeased but do not complain. They refuse me permission to correct my errors and thus improve my service.

How far you go in life depends on your being tender with the young, compassionate with the aged, sympathetic with the striving, and tolerant of the weak and the strong. Because some day in life you will have been all of these.
–George Washington Carver

☆ ☆ ☆ ☆ ☆

"A man takes contradiction and advice much more easily than people think, only he will not bear it when violently given, even if it is well-founded. Hearts are flowers; they remain open to the softly falling dew, but shut up in the violent downpour of rain."
–Richter

☆ ☆ ☆ ☆ ☆

Happy is the man who has learned to hold the things of this world with a loose hand.

☆ ☆ ☆ ☆ ☆

Successful people who motivate themselves and others are aware of and *honestly* identify their motives--or those of the ones they would motivate--and then take the action steps necessary for success. Good managers encourage others to take the steps necessary for their personal success!
-Zig Ziglar

☆ ☆ ☆ ☆ ☆

Dr. Norman Vincent Peale: "The trouble with most of us is that we would rather be ruined by praise than saved by criticism."

Commitment . . .

"There is a big difference between being interested in achieving a special goal and being committed to it. Committed people stick to their agreements. People merely interested in a goal have some reason for not achieving it—the time's not right or the plan was no good to begin with. The Sales Rep who merely hopes for improved sales, the factory foreman who only tries to increase production are defeated before they begin. But for people who have made the decision to achieve—the commitment to achieve—there are no such things as mumbled excuses. Their goals aren't finessed or negotiable. They are fiercely and single-mindedly pursued. If you really want to get something done, decide to do it—commit to your commitment. And your objectives will soon become your accomplishments."

Ken Blanchard

☆ ☆ ☆ ☆ ☆

MANAGEMENT MAXIMS TO LIVE BY...

1. Have a purpose firmly in mind and minimize ambiguity.
2. Do your homework – see both the big picture and understand the details.
3. Surprises are a cardinal sin. Strategic planning must become a way of life.
4. Know your customers and their needs. Know them as individuals and listen with both ears.
5. Make decisions. Take risks. Learn from your mistakes and live with change.
6. Always wear the 'company hat'. Keep in mind what is in the best interest of the company as a whole.

   – This is the personal managerial roadmap of Reginald Jones, CEO, General Electric

> "The best executive is the one who has sense enough to pick good men to do what he wants done, and self-restraint enough to keep from meddling with them while they do it."

☆ ☆ ☆ ☆ ☆

I, THE AMERICAN BUSINESSMAN...

I bring together ideas and people.

I organize talents and resources.

I create products and opportunities that expand the human potential.

I make dreams a reality.

I am a survivor, overcoming obstacles every minute of every day, learning from each failure and growing stronger with every success.

I am a builder, developer and lover of hard work, loyalty, honesty and determination.

I am a doer, a dreamer, and an opportunity creator.

I am an inventor and an innovator.

I am an AMERICAN BUSINESSMAN.

☆ ☆ ☆ ☆ ☆

Happiness is a delicate balance between what one is and what one has.
J. H. Denison

SIGN ON A RECEPTIONIST'S DESK:

```
Answers.....$1.00

Answers that require thought.....$2.00

Correct Answers.....$4.00

Dumb looks are still free.
```

☆ ☆ ☆ ☆ ☆

THAT'S NOT MY JOB

This is a story about four people named Everybody, Anybody, Somebody and Nobody. There was an important job to be done and Everybody was sure that Somebody would do it. Anybody could have done it, but Nobody did it. Somebody got angry about that because it was Everybody's job. Everybody thought Anybody could do it, but Nobody realized that Everybody wouldn't do it. It ended up that Everybody blamed Somebody when Nobody did what Anybody could have done.

☆ ☆ ☆ ☆ ☆

The great trouble today is that there are too many people looking for someone else to do something for them. The solution for most of our troubles is to be found in everyone doing something for himself.

Henry Ford

Daily Exercise for the Non - athletic

Making the rounds is a calorie guide citing a recent medical association report: "Proper weight control and physical fitness cannot be attained by dieting alone. Many people who are engaged in sedentary occupations do not realize that calories can be burned by the hundreds by engaging in strenuous activities that do not require physical exercise."

Here's the guide to calorie-burning activities and the number of calories per hour they consume:

Activity	Calories
Beating around the bush	75
Jumping to conclusions	100
Climbing the walls	150
Swallowing your pride	50
Passing the buck	25
Throwing your weight around (depending on your weight)	50-300
Dragging your heels	100
Pushing your luck	250
Making mountains out of molehills	500
Hitting the nail on the head	50
Wading through paperwork	300
Bending over backwards	75
Jumping on the bandwagon	200
Balancing the books	25
Running around in circles	350
Eating crow	225
Tooting your own horn	25
Climbing the ladder of success	750
Pulling out the stops	75
Adding fuel to the fire	150
Wrapping it up at the day's end	12

☆ ☆ ☆ ☆ ☆

The most important single ingredient in the formula of success is knowing how to get along with people.
THEODORE ROOSEVELT

TWO OUTSTANDING BOOKS
By LARRY BIELAT

WINNING WORDS
A BOOK OF MOTIVATIONAL AND INSPIRATIONAL QUOTATIONS

$8.00 PER COPY

"A book you will read over and over"

THIS BOOK IS TREASURED BY THOSE WHO USE IT

DUE TO THE TREMENDOUS RESPONSE TO "WINNING WORDS" WE HAVE A NEW BOOK

JUST OFF THE PRESS

WORDS of CHAMPIONS
THIS BOOK HAS BEEN PUBLISHED BY POPULAR REQUEST FOR MORE MOTIVATIONAL AND INSPIRATIONAL QUOTATIONS

$8.00 PER COPY

"A book you will use daily"

ANOTHER TREASURE OF WIT AND WISDOM

A 30 YEAR COLLECTION OF MOTIVATIONAL MATERIAL
PUBLISHED IN TWO SEPARATE BOOKS
SEND ORDER AND PAYMENT TO:

**ALL SPORTS ART & PUBLICATIONS
P.O. BOX 4399
EAST LANSING, MICHIGAN 48826**